Never ALONE

A STORY OF GOD'S FAITHFULNESS AND LOVE

Never Alone: A Story of God's Faithfulness and Love

Copyright © 2024 by K M. Leffler

For permissions contact: contact@kmleffler.com

Paperback ISBN-13: 979-8-9919309-0-1
Hardback ISBN-13: 979-8-9919309-1-8
Ebook ISBN: 979-8-9919309-4-9

Library of Congress Control Number: 2024924502

First Edition, 2024

Disclaimer: This book is nonfiction. I have changed and omitted some of the names of people and places within this book, to protect the privacy and identities of those involved. This book is based on my personal experiences and includes my personal views.

Edited by Jo Elizabeth Pinto
Cover Art Created By Rob Williams, Book Cover Designer

Scriptures taken from the Holy Bible, New International Version®, NIV®. Copyright © 1973, 1978, 1984, 2011 by Biblica, Inc.™ Used by permission of Zondervan. All rights reserved worldwide. www.zondervan.com The "NIV" and "New International Version" are trademarks registered in the United States Patent and Trademark Office by Biblica, Inc.™

Printed in Brighton, Colorado, USA

Published by Painted Arrow Books, (December, 2024)

Website: www.kmleffler.com

Never ALONE

A STORY OF GOD'S FAITHFULNESS AND LOVE

K. M. Leffler

Painted Arrow Books

Dedication

First and foremost, I dedicate this book to God,

without whom this book never would have

been written. I am grateful for His love, compassion,

and faithfulness in my life. He has always guided me,

even when I didn't know it.

To my family: my husband, and my children.

I love you all so much.

You are the light of my life every day.

Other Books by

K. M. Leffler

Ask. Seek. Knock.
A Prayer Journal

Complete Surrender
A Visual Prayer Journal

Table of Contents

Inspiring Hope through Faith.

*Find Hope, Discover Faith, Embrace Love
Through God and His promises.*

Hope through Love

Chapter 1

"For I know the plans I have for you," declares the LORD, "plans to prosper you and not to harm you, plans to give you hope and a future." – Jeremiah 29:11 (NIV)

"I know the plans I have for you, declares the Lord." Those words are important and powerful. They reassure us that God knows what is planned for our lives, and even more, that the plans He has for us are meant to give us hope and a future. This first verse tells us of God's faithfulness, that He will always be with us because He does have great plans for our lives. We may not always understand what those plans are, and our definition of "great" will certainly be different from God's idea of "great." But there's one thing we can be sure of. This verse guarantees God is always with us and always faithful, even when we can't see it.

Never Alone

I'm sure there have been times when you felt alone and hopeless, or maybe you feel that way now. However, no matter where you are right now, it's important to know that you are not alone, and there is hope.

Often we have experiences that leave us feeling helpless and hopeless. Some people have financial struggles, relationship difficulties, or health issues. They may feel like nothing is going right. No matter what they do, their troubles keep getting worse. They may not know where to turn or who to talk too. They may feel abandoned, separated from everyone and everything they know, and thereby hopeless and alone.

Others may experience a darkness that engulfs and suffocates them all at the same time. They feel isolated, trapped, and unable to breathe. They're desperate to break through the darkness, but they feel lost, like no one cares.

If any of these situations describe you now or have described you at some point, I want you to know there's hope.

I don't know if you believe in God, but I do. I believe God is the only one who can bring us peace when the waves of chaos crash down on us. He is the light within our darkness. He is always there with us, even when we feel alone. Most importantly, He can give us hope through His love.

You're probably thinking at this point, "Great. She's going to preach about God."

I promise, I'm not. I'm not going to "preach" about anything. I'm going to share my testimony and yes, it will center on God and what He has done for me. But it's up to you to decide what to do with what you learn through my story.

I'm not perfect; I've never claimed to be. I make mistakes. I've stumbled and fallen. I've lost my way time and again and gotten back on track. The fact is, this just shows I'm human. It shows I'm someone who has gone through hard stuff. I've walked in deep darkness, but God has led me through to the light.

My journey is far from over. I still experience hard times. I react in the moment and then, when that moment has passed, I turn to the one I know I can always count on. I turn to God. He reminds me every time that He is there. He knows how I work and yet, He gives me grace again and again. I don't deserve His grace; I don't deserve His love. But that's the beauty of grace because He decided in His Mercy that we all deserve it. That's why He gave us His Son on the cross.

When I find myself struggling and losing my way, I do three things. First, I turn on worship music and sing my heart out. Second, I pray. I pray with every part of my being, with every part of my heart and soul. Sometimes God answers my prayers, and sometimes He doesn't. But even when He doesn't, I know He hears me.

The third thing I've been doing, and I admit, this has been more recent than any other time in my life, is I dive into Scripture, into God's word. Truth be told, during the latest hardship I've been dealing with, I've been spending more time in my Bible than I ever have before.

These three things are important to my walk. They strengthen my faith and trust in God. They remind me that He is always with me. He is more powerful than any darkness I might face. He has never let me down, despite my own shortcomings (and there are many.) He has never abandoned me. Music, prayer, and the Bible help sustain my hope in Him and His everlasting love.

Whatever your view of God is, I have one prayer for this book and for you. I pray that if you believe in God, my experiences will help you find a new and deeper relationship with Him. If you don't believe, then I hope you will learn about God's love and how significant a relationship with Him is. Most importantly though, my prayer is that you realize you are never alone, and that there's hope through God's love.

From Ðarkness to Grace

Chapter 2

So do not fear, for I am with you; do not be dismayed, for I am your God. I will strengthen you and help you; I will uphold you with my righteous right hand. — Isaiah 41:10 (NIV)

My faith has played a very important part in my life since I was young. My story starts when I was a child. I'm the oldest child in my family. I was raised in Florida in a Christian home. I went to church every Sunday with my parents, and I had grandparents and uncles who loved me. I only remember bits and pieces from my early childhood. Most of what I know comes from stories my mom has told me or from documentation I've collected as an adult.

I'm sure you've heard stories about how people have experienced God in very profound ways. I can't say I've seen Jesus in my dreams, nor can I say I've died and visited with

Jesus, only to come back to life. But God saved my life when I was a child, and I experienced His presence.

I was a nonverbal child with learning disabilities and serious depression. I don't recall much from my preschool or early elementary years. What I do know is that I was nonverbal till the age of five, and I remember having speech therapy as a result. My first three years of school I've blocked out, with a few exceptions. My disability made it hard for me to focus, especially in school. I was called names by students and teachers. Between the ages of four and seven, I remember being called stupid and dumb and told I would never go anywhere in life. I had no friends, and I spent most of my time alone in my room at home when I wasn't in school.

I got sent to the principal's office so often at school, I developed anxiety whenever anyone in authority approached me. This could be a police officer or a teacher, or anyone I perceived as having a position of power. I want to make it clear that I wasn't a "bad kid." I was very well-behaved. My parents never hit me. In fact, I was loved dearly by both of my parents and the rest of my family. I was just a kid who had a disability, who didn't understand what was wrong with me or why people treated me so badly.

The treatment I endured was so difficult, my mom said I would cry and beg her not to send me to school. But that wasn't where it ended. When my mom tried to transfer me to another school, the staff at the public school I went to threatened to have me removed from the home and get my mom arrested. Thankfully, my mom did eventually place me into a private school, but sadly not till I was going into third grade. Prior to that, I was locked in a suffocating darkness I couldn't escape. That darkness almost claimed my life.

I was four or five years old when it happened. My mom told me later my depression was so bad, doctors said she should have placed me in an institution. I have the paperwork that lists the recommendation. My mom refused to abandon me that way. But that wasn't the worst part. I know it's hard to imagine a child of four or five feeling that taking her own life is the only way out. Children at that age are young and innocent, so to visualize one of them feeling so depressed and alone is hard to fathom. That thought alone can be heart breaking. Unfortunately, for me, it was true.

So true in fact, my mom told me she remembers me acting out my suicide with my barbie dolls. I honestly can't imagine being a parent and watching your child acting out such a thing with her toys. The thoughts that went through my mom's mind must have been extremely heartbreaking. As a parent myself, it would probably destroy me inside if I ever saw one of my children playing out his or her own suicide with dolls or toys. Sadly, that wasn't the end.

Before I go forward, I want to warn you, what you are about to read might be triggering for some. However, I need to share this, and I promise there is a light at the end of this story.

When I think about my childhood, there's one moment I will never forget. It was during this time that I first experienced God. This is that "profound" experience I mentioned at the beginning of the chapter. I hadn't given my life to God yet. I was four or five years old. I didn't fully understand God and what it meant to take that step. I went to church with my parents every Sunday, and I knew who God was, but I hadn't yet made a commitment in my life. As for this moment, it was a dark time for me, and frankly it was the darkest it has ever been. This was the day God saved my life.

I remember walking into our kitchen. My mom was home, but she was busy in another part of the house. I stood at the counter. To my right was the playroom where all the toys were, and to the left was the pantry and the way to the office. I recall standing at the counter, staring straight at the wall. I felt lost, depressed, trapped, engulfed in darkness. That darkness felt cold and frightening, like I was drowning in it, like it was cutting off my air. I knew I had loved ones who cared about me, but I still felt really and truly alone. I wanted those feelings to stop.

So, I stood, staring at the wall in front of me. Then, I reached into a drawer, and I remember slowly taking out a knife. I can't recall everything about the knife, but I remember it had a brown handle. The only brown-handled knives we owned were our steak knives. I remember quietly pulling the knife out of the drawer and staring at it. The only thing I knew at that point was I wanted the pain to end. I stood in that kitchen, and I very clearly recall holding that knife up and pointing the blade at myself. I had every intention of ending my life at that moment. Both of my hands were wrapped around the handle, and I just stared.

I can't explain exactly what happened, but I do remember it clearly. My hands started to shake. I was having a hard time holding the knife steady. There was no one around me; no one was there to stop me. I was, as far as I knew, completely alone.

Then I heard a voice--a male voice--speak to me. The voice said, *"No, it's not your time. You are meant for a great purpose."*

The voice was firm, but loving and compassionate. There was no judgement in the tone, and when I heard it, I felt an overwhelming warmth, love, and peace wash over me. I can't explain it, but as soon as that voice spoke, it was like the darkness around me started to lift. I remember standing there, then slowly laying the knife on the counter and walking away. I felt a peace I'd never felt before. I felt love and warmth I didn't think I deserved because I thought I was broken. For the first time in my life, I didn't feel alone.

I found out later that my mom was watching me from the pantry. She told me she needed to wait and see what I would do. Sure, she could have stepped in and stopped me, but she knew what she was doing. I firmly believe God kept her from interceding. If she had, God couldn't do what I needed at that time.

I still can't wrap my head around how a child so young could feel so much pain, and yet I lived it. Years later, I made the decision to give my life to God. But that experience in the kitchen changed my life in a huge way. I don't know what "great purpose" I'm meant to do, but I know God has a plan for me.

Fact is, I do have a disability, and because of that, I don't tend to see or understand things the same way other people do. What I usually need is someone telling me directly what to do, or I need to see some sort of a sign. I don't know or understand what my purpose is. Perhaps I have been doing it; perhaps I haven't done it yet. But I know this. When God speaks to you and tells you that you are meant for great things, great things will happen.

Suicide is a heartbreaking situation that hurts those who are left behind. For the people who make that desperate decision, it's even more heartbreaking because of the level of hurt they're feeling inside. I was only four or five years old. I don't claim to understand how God works or why He intercedes for some and not others. But I know that day He did for me. Maybe it was because I was so young. After all, Jesus said, "let the little children come to me." Another reason could also be that I was already raised in church to know who God is. Or perhaps my mom prayed for me, knowing I was struggling and already walking down a dark path.

Whatever the reason was, while I felt alone, I never was. God was there. He broke through the darkness that held me, and He gave me love and compassion. He saved my life that day, and to Him I owe everything. That day, God took me from darkness to grace.

Never Alone

Broken to Healed

Chapter 3

He heals the brokenhearted and binds up their wounds.

— Psalms 147:3 (NIV)

God's plans for my life were slowly starting to form. I didn't see it at the time, maybe because I was too wrapped up in my struggles and depression as a child. However, one thing I've learned is that God doesn't advertise when He is making changes in our lives. He doesn't put it up in neon lights for everyone to see. He usually moves quietly. But I promise, if we take a deep breath and look back, we'll see that God was working in our lives the whole time.

I knew my life began to change at a certain point. I can tell you when that was. I was blessed to have amazing teachers from third through seventh grade. Although I've credited them with saving my life, it was God who actually saved me. These teachers continued the work He started. Their role was to heal me and give me strength. God was always looking out for me. He guided everything my parents did to give me a chance in life. He knew what He was doing, and He was always there with me from the beginning.

My life began to change in third grade when my parents placed me in a private school. My mom told me her only goal for me that year was that she wanted the school and my teacher to focus on building my confidence. I don't remember much from my year there, but I do recall that my teacher, Ms. H., did the I CAN Program by Zig Ziglar. As part of the program, Ms. H. gave me two stuffed bees. They were hugging each other and had hearts on their antennae. I remember Ms. H. always reminding me that I CAN do things. I CAN do great things. I was amazing, special, and loved. She encouraged me, and she always had a smile on her face. She made me feel good about who I was, and she started my healing journey.

The next year, my parents placed me in another private school. I attended that school from fourth to seventh grade. What I didn't know at the time was that I was so far behind when I entered that school, I should have been held back. My mom told me the decision was made to keep me in the 4th grade because my test scores showed I had a high IQ. That school believed in me. The teachers worked with me that first year. Then for 5th grade, I was placed in their Special Education Program, which consisted of a smaller classroom of about ten students.

I also did their specialized therapy program, which was made up of games and activities that helped the left and right sides of the brain work together smoothly. I participated in these therapy sessions for the next three years. That program, plus the smaller classroom and the teachers I had, helped to take me from completely broken to healed.

My teachers at the private school showed me what a real teacher was supposed to be like and how a student was meant to be treated. My teacher in the 5th and 6th grades, Ms. M., worked with me one on one when I needed it. I recall lots of times when she would be eating her lunch while helping me with a math assignment.

By the end of my 6th grade year, two amazing things happened. First, I wrote a poem. This was a big deal because prior to that, I absolutely hated writing! However, thanks to the patience and kindness of the teachers I had and to the therapy program, I discovered that I really loved to write.

The second thing that happened during my 6th grade year was that I made a very, very important decision. That was the year I decided to give my life to God, to accept Jesus as my Lord and Savior.

I hadn't had that relationship with Him before, at least not in a committed way yet. I knew who God was and who Jesus was because of my time in church and school. However, that didn't mean I had accepted Jesus as my Lord and Savior yet. In spite of the fact that I hadn't committed my life to Him, God was still protecting me. He was still faithful to me and provided me with healing, all before I gave my life to him.

This is a testament to God's love for us. He loves us even when we haven't made the choice yet to love him. He loves us so much, He will provide us with healing when we need it. He will be faithful to us, even before we give our lives to Him. He does this because He wants us to see His power. He does this as a way to call us to Him, to show us exactly what He can do with our lives if we follow Him. Committing to God was the best decision I've ever made, but it wouldn't be the last time I would ever offer my life to Him.

After sixth grade, Ms. M. tutored me over the summer, to make sure I was ready for the next year. She drove an hour each way to my house to tutor me, and she never once complained. She did it because she knew I needed it. She did it because she knew I was worth it. She believed in me, which was why she poured her time into helping me see my potential.

When I went into 7th grade, I already had a new view I didn't have before. However, that view only grew with the help of my 7th grade teacher, Ms. J. I still remember a conversation she had with our class.

"I don't like being in special ed," one of the students complained. "It means we're stupid."

"You aren't stupid," Ms. J. said in a kind voice. "Listen. None of you are stupid. Being in this class gives you an opportunity your peers don't have."

"How do you figure?" the disgruntled student asked, perking up a little.

"Well—" Ms. J. smiled. "There aren't as many students in the room, so I can stop and help if one of you gets stuck on something, or we can spend extra time on a lesson as a class. Other teachers don't have those options."

As I listened to Ms. J, I realized something important. We weren't defined by our disabilities. In fact, I began to understand that we could choose to let our disabilities define us, or we could choose to define them instead. I made the decision that I was going to define my disability.

My time at that school did more than just heal me. It gave me courage and confidence. It helped me to see the potential I had within me. What I didn't realize at the time was how important that growth would be. God knew even then that my life had to change because I would need to be confident in myself, and I would need to be strong to face what would come next. My relationship with Him and my healing that took place gave me something even more important; it gave me peace. You know that peace that people talk about, peace beyond all understanding? I had that peace, and that peace would play a very important role in my near future.

Trials and God's Peace

Chapter 4

And the peace of God, which transcends all understanding,

will guard your hearts and your minds in Christ Jesus.

- Philippians 4:7 (NIV)

When I look back on those years, I realize God was preparing me for what would come next. He knew the trials I would have to face, and He knew how to get me ready for them. He understood I would have to be strong and courageous to face the next part of my journey. He saw what was coming and, no, it wasn't easy at times. He gave me the tools and the faith to face my own Goliaths.

Unfortunately, we have to go through trials for a reason. Our challenges make us stronger in our faith. They allow God to mold us into who we are meant to be.

Never Alone

My high school years found me and my family in Colorado, and I faced new hardships. One of those was a repeat of what I went through in Elementary School. However, this time would be different. This time, I had God's love and strength on my side.

Many people think all teachers are there to support their students, but sometimes that isn't the case. I had a Special Education Teacher in High School. We'll call him Mr. N. Interestingly, I actually tested out of the Special Education program during High School. However, I was still allowed access to the supports if I needed them. Unfortunately, this also meant Mr. N. would be my academic advisor. As such, he had the final say on any classes I signed up for. Mr. N. made sure I was never placed in any regular math classes. In fact, I was placed in a class that taught basic math, including how to balance a checkbook. This was great, but it did nothing to prepare me for college, which was my goal.

One afternoon during my Senior year, Mr. N. walked into the Special Education room and found me looking at colleges. I can still remember that conversation today.

Mr. N. looked at me curiously. "What are you doing."

"Looking at a list of colleges. I need to see where they're located and who offers the program I want to go into," I answered in a nonchalant tone.

Mr. N. narrowed his eyes at me. "Kelly, you have no business looking at colleges. You won't make it. YOU belong in a technical school instead."

His words shocked me. He, of all people, was supposed to support and encourage me. After all, I had been on the honor roll multiple times during my high school years. This was the same mindset I had faced in elementary school, only now I wasn't that little girl lost in the darkness. Now I was a strong young woman God had healed, and I had no intention of allowing Mr. N. to walk all over me.

I stood up straight and looked right at my adversary. "Mr. N., I'm going to college, and I will succeed."

And then without another word, I immediately walked out of the room.

A few months later, I had to pick my last semester of classes. For me, going to college was important, but I wasn't prepared for it because I hadn't taken any required math classes. So, in an attempt to get ready, I chose a Pre-algebra class.

Mr. N. told me, "If you take this class, you'll fail, and I won't sign off on this for you to fail a class."

Once more, I was undeterred by his comments. I went home and told my mom what was happening and of course, she got involved. I'm thankful she did because I was able to take that class for my last semester of high school.

With God's help, I not only passed the class with an A, but I also won an award. It felt good to pass my class and win an award; I felt pride in my accomplishment. However, I credit God for my success because I wouldn't have been able to get through the class without His help. He was there when I took my class, and He was there when I had to get help from my mom. I never thought at any time I was alone because my faith was strong then. God hadn't brought me that far just so I could fall to the lies the devil was throwing at me. With God's help, I was able to show Mr. N. that underestimating me was the wrong decision. I was done being a victim of my past. I knew I was strong and smart, and I could do anything as long as God was by my side.

The second trial that took place during my high school years was the separation and divorce of my parents. It's hard as a kid to watch your home fall apart. It's even harder when you get dragged into the middle of it. However, despite how I felt about my parents' divorce, I remained focused on my classes and schoolwork. On one hand, it was a struggle, and there were times I felt alone and unheard. Other times, I didn't care. I had a peace about what my parents were going through because I saw them as adults who needed to deal with their own issues. I always had my faith even then, and I trusted God more than ever to help me get through those times. If it wasn't for His peace, that peace beyond all understanding, I know I wouldn't have gotten through everything the way I did.

The hardest part was the betrayal I felt from my church. When my dad moved out, he rented a room from a woman who would later become my stepmom. While I have a better understanding now as an adult, my view then was very skewed. However, I truly believe God used this time to show me something important.

The church we attended never said or did anything about the fact my dad showed up every week with the woman who would become my stepmom. It was hard for my family to see them together, and it did nothing to make me feel welcomed. Of course, a lot of my views of that situation came from my mom's influence. She wasn't necessarily right. The situation between my parents was and is still between them.

But at the time, I felt alone and betrayed by the church where I was supposed to feel welcome.

It didn't take long before I decided I didn't need to go to church to be close to God. I wasn't sure how I knew I was making the right decision; I just felt I was. While the situation of feeling betrayed hurt, the decision to walk away from the church came with peace. I was ok with it because I knew all I needed to have my relationship with God was my faith and knowing His word. Oddly enough, that feeling of betrayal came with its own lesson and growth.

When I look back on that time, I realize God used that to prepare me for what would happen many years later when the pandemic hit. During the pandemic, my family couldn't attend church because of the lockdowns. It never phased me once. I knew we would be okay, and when the time came, we would return to church.

God knows everything about us. He knows what the future looks like, and He sets things up to happen in order to prepare us for those future events. We don't see it, especially when we are caught in the moment, but when we look back, the lessons are there. God was molding and shaping us all along. Sometimes it's bit by bit, other times its more drastic. But no matter what, He acts to strengthen our faith, proving that He is always with us, walking beside us, holding us in His arms and waiting for us to trust Him in full surrender.

Never Alone

Lost in a Storm

Chapter 5

Immediately Jesus reached out his hand and caught him.

"You of little faith," he said, "why did you doubt?"

- Matthew 14:31 (NIV)

I would like to say by the time I moved out in 1999, my faith in God was strong and unbreakable. Unfortunately, that wasn't the case. Remember I told you I'm human, and I make mistakes. This part of my journey is an example of that. While I still believed in God, my faith was slipping. Sadly, I didn't know it, nor could I see it happening. I went through some hard times, but God would remind me later that year how important I was to Him.

In 1999, I found myself needing to get away. Things were rough at home, and college was becoming stressful. I needed a break. So, with my dad's help, I moved to Denver and rented a room from a friend of his. I got a job at the local mall selling shoes. The first store I started at didn't work out. So, I moved onto another store, still selling shoes. I was also secretly engaged to my boyfriend at the time. I spoke to my fiancé often via letters and phone calls, but after a while of living in Denver, I was still struggling with my job and family situations. My choice to move to Denver caused problems between my mom and me. I was really wrestling with my life choices.

Eventually I decided I needed to regroup and think about what I was going to do. My job wasn't working out. My boss thought it was funny to sexually harass me. When he didn't quit, I did. There was also the strained relationship with my mom and my sister I needed to repair. I wasn't sure if I would go back to school or move home, but I knew I needed to figure out a solution. I needed time to think, and unfortunately, my fiancé couldn't support me and broke up with me.

I felt completely hopeless and alone. My faith was severely wavering, and I felt lost. I decided, to stay in Denver and move to a friend's place, but things didn't get better.

I developed a health issue with low blood sugar. I struggled with the adjustment to what was happening in my body. I couldn't get my blood sugar to regulate, and it eventually interfered with me holding down a job. I discovered I needed access to snacks and water to keep my blood sugar up, or else I would get really sick and pass out. Unfortunately, employers wouldn't accommodate my needs. So, I spent more time unemployed than I did working.

I eventually met someone new. I'll call him Tim. As it turned out, Tim wasn't who he said he was. During a date night, three things came out. The first was Tim's view of women. He felt he had a right to treat a woman any way he wanted, even if it meant hitting her. I foolishly decided to overlook that big red flag. I didn't think there would ever be a problem, and I was sure I could hold my own if there was.

Then he attempted to rape me. Sadly, he got close to succeeding. But when I screamed for him to stop, he did, although I think the only thing that stopped him was that I had a friend nearby. While I was thankful that Tim didn't rape me, that moment left me shaking. I didn't feel good about myself. I knew I needed to end the relationship. The seed was planted in my mind, but for some reason, I needed an extra push to do it.

The third issue came after the attempted rape. It turned out to be the push I needed to call off the relationship. Tim and I were sitting at dinner when he admitted to me that he had a wife and a son. He told me he was separated from his wife and wanted to be with me. I was shocked because when I met him, he, a friend, and his dad had all told a friend of mine and me that he was single.

After his confession, I knew the relationship was over. I didn't support cheating, and I didn't want to be the "other woman." So, I made the decision that I had to end the relationship. However, Tim made that hard for me. He began to act strange and refused to see me or even talk to me, except when he felt like it. Even then, we never did talk or meet. He started to spend time with his wife again and told me he wanted to reconcile with her. He said I needed to leave him alone, which was odd because he was the one who contacted me multiple times. I had only reached out to him once after he confessed, to tell him the relationship was over. That was when I found out he intended to reconcile with his wife.

I made the decision to stop contacting Tim, but he kept reaching out to me. We met one evening to talk. I hoped to tell him we were through and walk away. I was tired of being harassed, tired of the games he was playing. When we met, though, he blamed me for everything.

I walked away that night, partly relieved the relationship was finally over. But I also felt betrayed, angry, hurt, and alone. That was the night I started a horrible habit. I began smoking. Looking back, I realize it was at this point I lost my focus on God.

I completely forgot He was there. I wish I could say that was the last I ever heard from Tim, but it wasn't. While I moved on, he continued to leave messages for me, wanting to talk and begging me to take him back. I ignored him. it was all I could do.

A month later, I met someone else. I'll call him Josh. When I met him, I found out he was from my home state of Florida. At one point, I had a chance to meet his sisters and his parents. Josh was in the military, and I figured I would give him a chance. It wasn't long before things went south again. Once more, there were warning signs.

The first one took place after I found out my aunt had passed. I had an asthma attack, but I had it under control. However, Josh threatened to call an ambulance if I didn't go to the hospital willingly for treatment. I reluctantly agreed to go. At the hospital, I found out Josh told the doctor I needed to be admitted because he believed me to be suicidal. Luckily, I was able to convince the doctor that wasn't the case, and it wasn't. As for Josh, I chalked it up to the fact that he was concerned about me, but the incident didn't sit right with me.

The second red flag was when Josh questioned me about the songs I was singing along with in the car. I'm a country girl, and I love singing to music, especially country songs. Unfortunately, Josh didn't like me singing to some of the songs and began to question me about my "loyalty" to him. He believed me singing certain songs meant I was cheating on him or planning to. In reality, they were just songs by my favorite artists. I shrugged the incident off as well, believing he was reading too much into the songs, and it was only a misunderstanding.

The final issue that happened ended our relationship. I bought him a present for his birthday. It was a suggestion made by his sisters, who actually liked me. The gift was some cheap concert tickets for a country band that was going to be in town. Unfortunately, he didn't like me buying him the tickets.

"You need to quit being obsessed with me!" he yelled. In the next instant, he grabbed my wrist and shoved me backward into the wall. "I'll never marry you!"

I was stunned. Marriage was never on my mind. All I wanted to do was get Josh something fun for his birthday. The gift was his sisters' idea, and they helped me pick it out. However, after his reaction, I took the tickets and left.

Both relationships left me feeling alone, worthless, and helpless. I never reported Tim to the authorities. I was too ashamed. I never reported Josh, either. At the time, I didn't see the point. Besides, I felt like I had done something wrong, like what I was experiencing was some sort of punishment I deserved. To be honest, I thought I was being punished for what happened between my fiancé and me. My fiancé blamed me for the destruction of our relationship. He accused me of breaking up with him when I didn't. So, I lived with this lie that our relationship ending was my fault, and these two incidents were the punishment I had to accept.

As I reflect on those events, I realize how badly I felt detached from God. Despite that feeling, I also realize something even more important. God was there through all of it. He was there when Tim tried to rape me and stopped. He was there when I found out he had a wife and son, and He gave me the strength and conviction to walk away. He was there when Josh tried to have me falsely committed to the mental ward. I know this because the doctor believed me over Josh, and I know in my heart that was God's doing. God was there when Josh grabbed me and shoved me against the wall. Things could have gone way worse than that, but they didn't. He saw me through that situation and overall kept me safe.

Yes, there were red flags, and it took me some time to catch on. Fact is, I tend to see the good in people. With Josh, I brushed off what happened at the hospital as a misunderstanding and the comments about me singing in the car as a bad day. But with Tim, I knew his actions were wrong. I may not have picked up on it after the rape, but I did after he told me he was married, and I had no desire to be the "other woman" to a man who was cheating on his wife.

When I think about these events, it reminds me of the story in the Bible where Jesus was walking on water, and he called to Peter to join him. Peter took the step of faith, but when he saw the waves crashing around him, he got scared. He lost his faith. His fear was so big, he couldn't keep his eyes on Jesus, who was standing right there.

When I look back on this time in my life, I realize I was much like Peter in the story. I was so overcome by the hardship that was piling up on me, I lost sight of Jesus and my faith. However, if you remember the rest of the story, Jesus was still there. As Peter began to sink into the waves of despair and fear, Jesus reached out his hand to save him. He never once abandoned Peter. He stayed right there on the water and waited for Peter to cry out for help. The moment he did, Jesus reached out to save him. Jesus brought to Peters attention that his fear and doubt were bigger than his faith. Peter removed his eyes from Jesus and, as a result, began to sink.

So many times, we find ourselves overcome by fear, despair, anger, loss, and sorrow. When we lose sight of Jesus, we start to fall beneath the waves of despair. This is the devil's plan; it's how he attacks us, and he does a good job of playing on our human emotions. But just like in the story, Jesus is still there. He is waiting for us to reach up and take His hand so He can pull us out of the waves and closer to Him. So, while I was losing my faith, while I felt alone and full of shame, God was close, waiting for me to reach out and remember His love. He didn't abandon me. Truth is, I was never alone. I had Him with me the whole time. I only needed to reach out and take His hand.

Never Alone

Returning to Him

Chapter 6

And we know that in all things God works for the good of those who love him, who have been called according to his purpose. – Romans 8:28 (NIV)

"In all things God works for the good of those who love him." These words are so true. God knows who we are, and He knows our hearts. In the stormiest of seas, God is there, much like Jesus was there for Peter when he began to doubt.

Sometimes God does things we don't expect, just to get our attention and to remind us He loves us endlessly. I'm grateful to know my God knows me. He's aware that I'm human, and I can be emotional at times, or I can get lost within the waves. Yet He is still there, and He still loves me. Talk about an awesome God, a Father with an endless amount of love and patience for His children. Otherwise, I fear what would become of us.

The devil's job is to attack us, to knock us down and harm us. But when we are saved and have a relationship with God, we can take comfort in knowing God will love us through everything. Even when it feels like things are getting worse, God is always there. He knows the deceiver is always working against us. So, God waits for us to return to Him, so He can comfort us and wrap us in His love.

I'm sure there are those who will say, "Well, God doesn't care about me. He's never there because bad things keep happening to me. If He cared about me, why doesn't He stop them?"

I believe that there are two reasons. The first is that God gave us free will. That means we get to make our own choices. God doesn't force us to do what He tells us to. Instead, He gives us the choice to make decisions for ourselves. In the same way that no parent can force a child to make the right decisions, God can't force us to make good choices. He lets us choose our own paths and suffer the consequences, hoping we will come back to Him.

My second reason is that as a parent, it's not possible for me to be with my kids all the time. So, when something bad happens to one of my children through no fault of his or her own, I can't always be there to stop it. However, I am always there waiting for my son or daughter to return to me, and when they do, I will wrap them in my arms and comfort them. Yes, I'll be scared for my children. Yes, I'll hurt because of what they've gone through. But I will always be there for them afterwards to help them and comfort them. It's the same with God. Sometimes the free will of others causes bad things to happen to us, and we are not to blame. But we can always rely on God to be there for us.

As children of God, the devil is always attacking us. It's what he does. He was given reign after Adam and Eve sinned. So, things do happen to us when we wish they wouldn't. The good news is, God is always there for us, wrapping us in His love.

Another argument I've heard over the years is, "God is supposed to be all-knowing and powerful. He can stop the devil if He wants, but He chooses not to."

However, when Adam and Eve sinned, God made it known we would live in sin and the consequences that come with that sin. There is good news, though. While sin has separated us from God and caused us to live in a world of pain and hardships, God sent His Son to redeem us. The death of Jesus on the cross and His resurrection from the tomb meant we can have a perfect relationship with Him. However, there's a catch. God won't force us to choose Him. That's our choice to make.

Finally, while God doesn't "let" bad things happen to us, He does let us go through storms. Sometimes it's because we make choices that lead to those storms. Sometimes it's because the devil attacks us. Then there are times when God uses the storms to help us grow, to increase our faith. Those storms can destroy us, or they can strengthen us. How we react to them is up to us. We can either choose to reach out to God and believe He will get us through, or we can blame Him and turn against Him for letting the storms happen.

Based on what I remember, I can honestly say I've never once blamed God for anything bad that has happened to me, nor have I ever said, "don't you care about me?" Instead, I've always gone to Him sooner or later, told Him how I'm feeling, and asked Him to help me through the trial. I ask because I have faith that He will help me if I ask. I know I'm weak, but He is strong, and as the Bible says, His strength is made perfect in our weakness.

This is where my story picks up. Not long after the last incident with Josh, I decided to sell my concert tickets. I figured someone could use them, and I needed the money. So, a friend of mine suggested that I go to her friend's house to sell my tickets. There was supposed to be someone there who would be interested in them.

At her friend's house, I met a guy who wore blue Wranglers, a nice dress shirt, cowboy boots, and a cowboy hat. We hung out at first, till I got anxious and decided to step outside for a cigarette. The cowboy followed me outside.

He looked at me curiously. "So I hear you have some concert tickets to sell?"

I gave him a quiet nod. "Yep, I do. Alabama tickets for Fiddlers Green."

"How much do you want for them?"

"Only what I paid. Fifty bucks."

He smiled. "Well, I'll take them, on one condition. You have to go with me."

I was stunned, to say the least. I'm sure my jaw hit the ground, or at least it felt like it did. I definitely wasn't looking for another relationship yet, but I didn't think it would hurt to go to the concert anyway. The cowboys name? I'll call him Matt.

I went with Matt to the concert, and not long after, I moved in with him. Matt made me laugh; he made me smile. He treated me respectfully, like a real gentleman should. He looked out for me and constantly tried to do things for me. He really cared about me. A month or two later, we moved to Idaho Springs. We were living there when I started making plans to go home to Florida for Christmas, and Matt decided to join me.

For New Year's Eve, we stayed on the beach in Daytona. First, he took me out for dinner at a nice restaurant. Then we walked on the beach to ring in the New Year.

When the clock struck 12 and the fireworks went off, Matt knelt down, pulled out a gold band with a small heart-shaped amethyst stone, and proposed. I was speechless. All I could do was cry and nod yes until I could find my voice. Oddly enough, I knew this was coming, but I didn't know when. A month earlier, he bought the ring, and he was so worried I wouldn't like it that he showed it to me.

After we returned home, we moved into my dad's house for a short time. We set our wedding date for July of 2000. But unfortunately, my fear and anxiety took over. I didn't have a reason to question whether or not Matt loved me. He always took care of me and made sure I was happy. We both were happy, actually. It was the first time I felt safe with a guy, but my fear and anxiety from my previous relationships haunted me.

I left my dad's house for a hotel room. I needed space. I was scared, and I didn't know what to think. My anxiety skyrocketed. Terrible thoughts raced through my mind. *How could Matt love me? What if he decided I was too broken later? Would he still want to be with me? What if he left me?* It was most likely the devil planting those thoughts.

Matt called me at the hotel room, wanting to know where I was. He asked if we could talk, then came to the hotel. As if God was listening to my heart and knew what I needed, Matt told me he loved me and would never hurt me. He knew about my previous relationships and how bad they'd gone, but he still loved me. Matt reassured me I had nothing to worry about and promised me I would be safe with him.

After our conversation, I felt a sense of relief wash over me, and those thoughts I was having disappeared. God was looking out for me; He knew what I needed to hear. I truly believe God brought Matt into my life for a reason.

After everything I went through prior to Matt, God was there to comfort me and let me know I was worthy of love. As the verse says, "In all things God works for the good of those who love him. He worked out something good, someone to love me, someone to care for me and restore my faith.

Matt and I got married, and it's a decision I don't regret making. I'd like to say we never had any hardships, but we did and still do. We went through a major trial that tested both of us and our marriage. However, I can say because of God, we've been married for twenty-four years at the time of this writing. Thank you, God, for your love, grace, and faithfulness.

Precious Gifts

Chapter 7

Children are a heritage from the LORD, offspring a reward from him. -Psalms 127: 3 (NIV)

Being mothers is one of the most precious gifts God can give us. He created women to carry babies in their wombs, to protect them and to be nurturers. He gave us the gift of bringing life into this world. Therefore, it's up to us to provide our children with love, nurturing and guidance. Being a mother is more than just a gift, though. It's a miracle! Those precious hands and feet, the small facial features we get to see every day; we get to watch them as they grow.

More than that, the minute we find out we're pregnant, we tend to dream about what our children's lives will be like. What kind of future they will have. In this way, it's like we get a small glimpse into how God sees us as His children. When we become a parent, we are filled with an unconditional love and bond to our children. That same unconditional love is exactly what God has for us. God has entrusted us with the care of a life He has blessed us with, and that's a big honor.

As parents, we also understand we can't always protect our children. We can't regularly help them when they are in trouble. I imagine this must be how God feels when we experience hardships and tough times. He won't always stop them from happening, but He will always be there for us, no matter what. Becoming a parent is a gift beyond just giving birth to a child. It's a chance to, in some small way, view ourselves from God's perspective.

It was 2001, and thankfully my faith had regrown to where I was praying a lot more than I had in previous years. This became a blessing, because as it turned out, I had to rely on my faith when I became pregnant that year with our first child. Unfortunately, my pregnancy didn't go well. I was extremely ill with hyperemesis gravidarum (or severe morning sickness), and eventually I was placed on bed rest.

I was working at the time, and I ended up losing my job. To make it worse, my emotions were all over the place. As women, we know our hormones are elevated during pregnancy, and mine definitely were. I found myself crying, often worried and anxious. It didn't help that Matt and I were already under stress. Our vehicles were being broken into regularly, and there was some tension in our marriage as well. So, I did what I knew to do. I prayed every day that God would make my daughter healthy and help me through the pregnancy. Eventually my sickness got better as I approached my due date.

After my daughter "Angel" was born, my instincts told me something was wrong. Every time I tried to pick her up, she would scream as if she were in pain. I couldn't calm her no matter what I did. Those struggles wore on me, and I ended up with postpartum depression. I did get help, and I got better, but I also found my peace in my prayers with God. Unfortunately, my instincts were right. I quickly discovered the only time I could touch my daughter was when she was swaddled in a blanket. If she wasn't, she would scream.

By the time she was two, I learned there were other concerns. Angel started to run out of our apartment. I had to lock all the doors to prevent her from leaving. She wasn't at all interested in her toys. She was also nonverbal. But it was what happened one afternoon that really made me worry.

Angel wanted something to eat. She couldn't tell me what she wanted, but she tried. So, I decided to have her show me, and I followed her to the kitchen. I watched as she went to the fridge. At first, I thought she was going to open the door. Instead, I watched curiously as she placed both her hands on the door. However, my curiosity changed to horror, because the next thing she did shook me to the core. Angel pulled her head backwards and went to slam it into the fridge. Luckily, I was able to stop her before she did. I carried her back to the living room and held her close to me as I rocked her back and forth. After she calmed down, I sat her on the floor and turned her around so I could look at her. At that moment, every dream I had for her, every hope I had for her future, disappeared. The pain in her eyes shattered my heart. Something was wrong with my daughter, and I knew it.

It wouldn't be till much later that we would find out Angel is autistic, and at the time, had an intellectual disability. During her toddler, preschool, and elementary years, all we knew was that things weren't going well. Her physical aggression increased. In fact, by the time she was in the fourth grade, I got a phone call every day from the school to pick her up. At that point, I was in school myself and raising our second child.

A month or two before the end of Angel's fourth grade year, I had to pull her out of school. The report about the latest incident indicated to me that the school was instigating the events that caused her to react aggressively.

The principal looked me straight in the eye and told me coldly, "Ms. Leffler, if you can't discipline your daughter, I'll do it for you."

As a mother, I took his words and his tone as a threat, a threat from someone who both my child and I were supposed to be able to trust. It was like I was seeing my time in elementary school playing out all over again, only this time it was with my child. Needless to say, I didn't waste any time removing my daughter from the situation. We got her tested a month later, and that was when Angel received her diagnoses of Autism with an intellectual disability.

I wish I could say things improved after the diagnoses, but they didn't. We made agreements with the schools during IEP (Individual Educational Plan) meetings, only for those agreements to be broken by the schools. We asked for our daughter to be placed in a different school district, but our requests were denied. In middle school, we asked that Angel be transitioned from class to class after passing periods were over, which was refused at first. It wasn't till she had multiple breakdowns from the sensory overload of going through the halls with throngs of noisy, jostling students that the school finally conceded on even that minor point.

It didn't take long until Angel began refusing to go to school, which only caused more physical aggression at home. I remember a specific time when the middle school overstepped. I received a call from her teacher. She asked me if she and the resource officer (a local policeman) could come to our home and talk to Angel because she was refusing to go to school. The teacher assured me that if she still refused, they wouldn't force her. I agreed to let them come, thinking I was doing the right thing.

At first, the teacher and the resource officer spoke with Angel about how important it was for her to attend school, and yet she still refused. When their talking did no good, what happened next horrified me. They grabbed Angel and literally carried her out of my home. I watched helplessly as she screamed. I was told not to intervene and not to follow them. Instead, I stared in horror as they dragged her out the door, one by the legs and the other by the arms. They carried her to the officer's car that way and put her in. As they went to drive away, Angel got her door open and hung halfway out of the car. And to make everything worse, I got a call later to pick her up because they couldn't manage her.

Not long after, we had an emergency IEP meeting. It was Halloween, and I'll never forget that day. I showed up with my advocate. We knew things weren't working, and we planned to request out-of-district placement again. Unfortunately, the meeting went bad very quickly. Angel found out I was there, and it didn't take long before she attacked me in the conference room, right in front of her teacher, the principal, and the district staff. They all watched calmly, completely stone-faced, and did nothing as my daughter physically attacked me in that meeting.

My advocate was the only one who tried to help get her off of me. Eventually, my daughter and I left the room and the school. Within 20 minutes, my advocate met me in the parking lot and told me we'd been given out-of-district placement, the very thing we'd asked for at the start of the school year. Unfortunately, the damage I'd hoped to avoid had already been done.

Over time, we got multiple services put in place for Angel, but none of them worked for her. There were several times she ended up in one residential facility or another, usually only for a day or two because of Medicaid's policies. However, once she stayed for several months.

It happened right after the IEP meeting when she attacked me. She ended up in a facility and thankfully, we got a caseworker who went to bat for us. He told Medicaid Angel could not be sent home after three days. She needed to stay in the facility long enough for the staff to see her aggressive behavior. He did this because he saw how badly injured I was. I had bruises and bloody scratches all over my arms. Medicaid gave our caseworker the time and sure enough, Angel gave them reason to hold her in the facility for four months, from November to February.

While she was there, we went through family therapy. It was difficult being away from my daughter like that. It was one of the hardest experiences we had to deal with.

When Angel came home, she began refusing to attend school again. I did everything I could to work with the district, asking for help with the situation. The district tried to take us to court for truancy. According to our original agreement with the district, we had till February to get our daughter back in school. In spite of the fact that we stayed in constant communication with the district, we were served with court papers on the first day of Thanksgiving break with only 2 weeks to find a lawyer before the court date.

We were thankfully able to get a lawyer on short notice, with the help of my dad. The lawyer took the case and quickly got it dismissed. Apparently, the district never told their lawyer they were taking the parents of a severe needs child with an IEP to court. He literally thought he was dealing with a juvenile delinquent. So, when my lawyer contacted him, he was shocked and dropped the case. We did have to go through mediation to work out the situation, but the district realized at that point, we were serious about protecting our rights and our child.

Throughout the long ordeal, I found myself praying a lot. I prayed for help and guidance. God answered when we got an advocate, and He answered when we needed a lawyer on short notice. But the worst part was that I felt I had somehow failed my daughter. That's the most defeating feeling ever. I also felt alone, as it was me who had to be on the front lines. My husband worked long hours to keep our home going while I was left managing the medical appointments, the IEP meetings, and the day-to-day school issues. I had to deal with the meltdowns at home, all while caring for a toddler. At one point I thought it was a punishment I had to endure because I blamed myself for my daughter's disabilities, but God reminded me that wasn't true.

As bad as things might have ever seemed, there are two gifts that came from this. The first is Angel. She's now an adult, and she is doing well. Those hard days are behind us now, and for that I am thankful. She's strong and amazing. She never finished high school, but she did get her GED. In fact, at the time of this writing, we plan to go watch our daughter graduate in June. An event, that at one time, I was sure we wouldn't get to see. Both my husband and I couldn't be prouder of her. She has a lot to learn yet, and I pray she'll find her way to God, but she is thriving. My baby girl, the child I call Angel girl, is slowly proving she defines her disability instead of letting it define her.

The second gift from God that came from this is the love and friendship I received. While we lost a lot of people in our lives, we gained the important ones, the ones that stayed around for the long haul. I am most grateful for them. One person I met was a woman named Chris. I met her at the local MOPS (Mothers of Preschoolers) group, and we became friends. When I think about those times, when I think about the ones who stood by me, it was Chris who was there. Even when she saw firsthand what we had to deal with, she never judged us. She was always there when I needed to talk or needed a friend. God gave her to me, along with another friend of mine, a woman named T.D., who also has always been there when I needed someone to talk to. I met her at the same MOPS group.

The only other friends I had were Dayna and Charisse, the two friends I'd been able to count on since high school. Even if it was just a phone call, they were always there for me. All of these amazing people were there for us. My family and I knew we were surrounded in prayers often.

Between their friendship, prayers, and support, along with my return to church years before my daughter's diagnoses, I found the strength to keep fighting. I was able to maintain my faith in God and keep going every day. I could feel God's love around me, even though I felt scared and at times alone. He was there, doing His work like He had done all those times before. He brought important people into my life, people He knew I needed. Aside from my husband and my children, my friends were and are the most precious of gifts I could have ever asked for. So, for that, I can't express how extremely grateful to God I will always be.

Never Alone

More Precious than Gold

Chapter 8

Carry each other's burdens, and in this way you will fulfill the law of Christ. – Galatians 6:2 (NIV)

God has reminded me many times that He loves me, and He is always watching over me. Still, it always amazes me when I look back at my life and I notice how perfect His timing is. We may not see it at the time, but He is always working for our good. His will can play out in many different ways, but have you ever noticed how His timing works when he brings people into our lives?

As humans, we tend to search out relationships with others. We put value in the number of people we have in our lives, believing the bigger our circle is, the more support or love we have. However, God reminds us that it's not about the quantity of people we have in our lives, but the quality of the people who surround us.

I grew up in a family where I was loved and supported. I was always surrounded by people I knew I could count on. My parents were always there for me, despite our differences and the hardships that came and went. My mom fought for me during my school days. She did her best to protect me and help me grow. I recall my dad helping me with my homework. He also pushed me and asked the hard questions I needed to be asked. I also have a younger sister, who has been there for my children and me.

When it came to my kids, my parents were always there. My mom was there to help with Angel and Dustin. At one point, we got Angel to where she would attend school full time. Her physical aggression calmed down, too. Unfortunately, this only lasted for a year or two. By the time she entered high school, things began to get worse again. Her aggression turned from physical to verbal, and she began refusing to attend school once more. It was then that my mom took over the care of Angel.

My dad was a listening ear when I needed to talk. He helped us get a lawyer when the school district came after us. My sister was always ready to help, too. She would take Angel for visits. This allowed my husband and me, and our daughter, to have a break from each other when we needed it most. My family has been a blessing throughout my life and the lives of my kids, and for that I am grateful.

I have also had the blessing of loving grandparents, two of the most amazing people I could ever ask for. My grandma was my inspiration as a child. I loved going to her house, playing on her piano and singing with her. She always listened, even when she didn't have the answers, and she never judged me. My grandpa let me sit in his chair and help with his hunting dogs. When I asked to go driving, he would have me sit on his lap while we drove down the dirt roads in the national forest. I can still remember him encouraging me to keep the wheel straight and telling me what a good job I was doing. My grandparents were an anchor in my life. They encouraged me, supported me, and reminded me often how much I was loved.

I really didn't have many friends growing up. But when I went to high school, God placed two very special people in my life. They became my closest friends, and they're still very much a part of my life today. My friends Dayna and Charisse have always been there for me. There were times when I needed a shoulder, and they gave it. There were also times when they encouraged me and cheered me on. Even after high school, when we went our own ways, I knew I could still count on them.

If anything ever happened, all I had to do was pick up the phone and they would show up for me in a heartbeat. They've prayed for me when I needed it, and they've physically been there for me, too. They were and are more than just friends; they're sisters to me. God brought them into my life during high school because He knew I would need good friends by my side. They were the first true friends I ever had.

When my husband and I moved into our house, I had been a stay-at-home mom for a while. I had hardly any friends outside of Dayna and Charisse. For the most part, I'd been cut off from the outside world due to the needs of my daughter. I never had regrets about the time I spent at home raising her. My daughter needed me. But it came at a cost for me, although it was a sacrifice I happily made for her.

Before moving to our house, I spent a little time in a mothers' group. So, when we moved in, I looked for another group near our home. The group was called "Mothers of Preschoolers," or MOPS for short. It's a Christian group designed for moms to gather and support each other while focusing on God. Luckily, I found a group just up the road from my house at a local church. I joined the group and slowly made friends. In fact, that's where I met both of my friends, T.D. and Chris.

When I got pregnant with my son, I was able to continue with MOPS. My involvement with the group began to stir up a desire in me I hadn't felt for a very long time. After years of avoiding a church, I started to feel a pull to return. God's ways really are mysterious and amazing. When I stepped away, I was okay with it. I knew I didn't "need" a church to have a relationship with God, and I was completely at peace with that. I did attempt to return after Angel was born. I even had a dedication for her at one point.

You might be wondering what a dedication is. It's not the same as a baptism. To put it plainly, a baptism is a personal commitment and a show of faith an individual chooses to make. A dedication is a commitment the parents and a church make to raise a child in God's truth.

In the end, my short time at church when Angel was a baby didn't feel right. I discovered I wasn't comfortable being there, as if it wasn't yet time for me to reconnect. So, I didn't return until I joined the MOPS group near my house. My time with those moms created the pull I needed.

God was doing His work in me and again, He knew what was necessary before I did. He led me to the MOPS group, which led me to two of my most precious friends and which caused me to return to church. For the first time in a very long while, I was happy to be back, and I felt comfortable where I was. Interestingly enough, my return caused my husband to give his life to God, and he joined me, which was something I never thought he would do. My son loved going to church, and he still does. My daughter, on the other hand, had a difficult time. Due to her sensory and autism struggles, Angel never felt as if she belonged. However, I pray every day that she will find her way to God.

Another positive effect of me returning to church was that my faith was strengthened in ways I can't explain. I even made the decision to rededicate my life to God. I prayed about that for months, and I found peace in doing so. I also made the decision to be baptized again. I don't know if this is considered necessary once you've given your life to God, but I felt it was something I needed to do. As always, I let God guide me in what He wanted, and that was something I felt strongly about. However, what I didn't know was that God had a reason for me returning to church. I would discover in the coming years that my return would become the anchor to God I would desperately need.

Faith like a Child

Chapter 9

Jesus said, "Let the little children come to me, and do not hinder them, for the kingdom of heaven belongs to such as these." Matthew 19:14 (NIV)

I know I said at the start I wasn't going to preach, and I'm not. These are just my thoughts on an important subject, what I believe it means and why I think it matters to both our daily lives and my story. I want to take a break and talk about having faith like a child.

First, I feel it's crucial for you to know that while these are my stories, I'm not writing this book. God is writing it. He is directing my chapters and my words. I planned out what I was going to put in this book, but as God does, He has changed those plans to what He wants me to write. I had 10 chapters laid out with what each chapter was going to be about. However, as

I started writing, those chapters have changed. My choice to put verses at the start of each chapter was something I felt strongly pulled to do; it wasn't my original idea. So, it's important for me to stop here and touch on this subject. I can't tell you why.

I'd like you to stop reading and take a moment to think about a couple of questions before you continue. Give it some real thought. There's no wrong answer. Feel free to write down your thoughts.

Do you know why we are called "children of God?" Do you understand what it means to be a child of God? Why is it so important to be childlike, and what does being childlike have to do with faith? Take a moment, think about this for a minute or two, and write down your answers if you want to. These questions are very important, and we all need to answer them because our answers affect our faith.

Here are my thoughts. First, I believe God is our Father. He is the Father who created us. He loved us before we were born. He always knew us and *knows* us now. He desires a relationship with us. He loves us unconditionally; He is our refuge and protection when we need it, and He is always there for us. He is the ultimate parent, and He calls to us like a parent calls to a child.

My second reason is we are called to be childlike. The Bible says that unless we become like children, we will never enter His kingdom. But why? Why do we need to become like children?

Well, picture a child you know. Children are innocent, curious and full of wonder. They see the world in ways we as adults have forgotten. Their level of belief is immeasurable. I mean, think about it. They can easily believe in a man flying around the world in one night on a sleigh pulled by reindeer to bring them all toys every year, or a bunny that shows up with goodies on Easter morning. They also believe in the goodness of people, even when they're proven wrong over and over again. Their faith is pure and innocent in every way possible. They don't need "proof." They just need something to believe in.

As a child, I was like most kids. I used to daydream about a fantasy world. In this world, good won over evil, there were princes and princesses, and "happily ever after" existed. These are the ideas and beliefs of a child, unaware of what the world can really be like. But what if these ideas aren't far off from what God has for us? We are called to be His children, and through Him, good overcomes evil. As children of the King, we are like princes and princesses and with Him, happily ever after does exist.

There's another important quality of being childlike. Children hang on every word people say, full of a desire to hear stories that capture their attention. That's normal; it's what being a child is all about. Kids are always full of wonder, innocence, and curiosity. Those traits as children allow them to ask questions adults don't usually bother with. It allows them to ask and answer those "what if" questions with the wonder of a child. In fact, there's one question I know every child has been asked at some point. It's a great "what if" question, and it allows children to use their wonder to explore the possibilities of the world around them.

The question is, "If you had a time machine, where would you go?" I was asked that once, and I knew exactly where I would want to go. Oddly enough, even as an adult, my answer is still the same. Sure, it's expanded, but the answer I had as a child hasn't changed. It was simple. If I had a time machine and I could go anywhere, I would want to go back in time and meet Jesus. I would want to sit at His feet and listen to His stories, listen to Him talk and ask Him questions. I would want to follow Him for a little while and watch Him perform His miracles. I don't need some sort of "proof" to know He existed or to believe in Him. But how absolutely perfect, amazing, and powerful it would be to experience His presence on earth!

I bring this up because our faith and trust in God needs to come from the place of a child, a place of pure, innocent belief. Children don't need proof that God is there; they just know. However, as adults, we get so wrapped up in our world, in our circumstances, that we can easily lose that belief. We get stuck on the idea of "proof" and "facts" in order to believe something to be true. We forget that we are children of God and that we are called to have faith as pure and innocent as that of a child, a child who believes in Him and trusts that He is with us. A child who is full of wonder and seeks out a relationship with Him because we want it and need it.

There's another reason why we are called to be childlike. As children, when our world starts to spin out of control, who are the first people we run too? Hopefully, we seek shelter within the love and protective embrace of our parents. As children of God, we should be running to Him as well. When it's storming and our world is appearing to fall apart, we need to run to God. We need to run to the shelter of His love and the protection of His embrace. God is always there; He is just waiting for us to take that step and to refocus our belief and our trust on Him. When the storm hits, He will reach out and grab our hand. He will be the light within our darkness. He will provide us with everything we need because He already knows what our needs are. His plans may not always make sense to us, just like the decisions of earthly parents may not always make sense to their children.

We *need* to want to sit at the feet of God, hanging on every word He says. We *need* to feel His love and protective embrace. We can't experience that physically, not yet anyway. However, there will come a time when we will be able to sit with Jesus and talk to Him and listen with all awe and wonder. Until that day comes, there are ways for us to seek Him out. We can start by reading our Bibles and by praying every day and opening our hearts to Him. We need to run to Him when things have gone wrong and most importantly, when things have gone right.

I didn't make it this far in my journey because I lost my faith. I had my faith the whole time. Did it become shaken? Yes. Did it waver? Of course. Did I lose my way at times? Certainly. But through everything that happened, I always had my faith deep down inside, and I never once blamed God for anything that went wrong in my life. Instead, I asked Him to help me. Sure, I questioned Him at times, because I wanted to understand and know why things were going wrong. But I never once blamed Him or completely turned away from Him. I always had my faith, and that's why I always made it through my storms, my rough walks, my lost paths. Even if that faith was shaky, I always had it. I'm thankful I did, because without it, I could have easily given up years ago.

I hope as you continue reading the rest of my story, you'll think about these questions. Where is your faith right now? What is your relationship with God about? Have you taken the time to look back on your past struggles and seen where God has been working? Do you BELIEVE He is always there with you? Do you believe you are never alone? For those who don't believe, why? What are you struggling with? Is there a storm that prevents you from seeing your worth in Him? Do you long for something more, but you don't know what? No matter what the question is or what the answer is, I know God is there to help us and to guide us, if we just have faith like a child.

Never Alone

My Trust is in You

Chapter 10

I will say of the LORD, "He is my refuge and my fortress, my God, in whom I trust." -Psalms 91:2 (NIV)

"In whom I trust." These are four very important words when we think about our faith. Trusting God is crucial if we hope to have a relationship with Him and if we hope to experience His love and peace. But trust isn't easy. It's hard enough to trust someone we can see every day. It's even harder to trust someone we can't physically see. However, our trust in God stems from our faith in Him. It comes from knowing His word and His promises to us and remaining focused on Him, even when the storm is beating down on us, even when the waves threaten to pull us under and suffocate us. It's that faith in God that allows us to trust Him.

When we can't physically see Him in human form, we can see His work before us. All we have to do is open our hearts. We can see the trees, mountains, animals, the love of two people, the innocent smiles and laughter of a child. Whether it's someone giving another food or helping a person across a street, God is there. He is compassion, love, mercy and grace, even when we think we are alone.

I talked about my experience with my daughter and with MOPS, but I haven't spoken about my son. There is hope in this story. I see this as a story of pure trust because it took trust to make the decision I had to make.

In May of 2009, I became pregnant again. We wanted a son. However, I knew after my last pregnancy, this time would be worse. Something in me told me this was not going to be easy, and it wasn't. Within weeks of finding out I was pregnant; I became sick with hyperemesis gravidarum again. At that time, my husband was working out of state. So, it was just Angel and me. I was a little scared, but I told myself I could handle what was coming. Unfortunately, I didn't know how bad things would get.

In June, I ended up in the hospital, severely dehydrated. The doctor decided taking medicine by mouth wasn't going to work well enough for me on its own. So, I was given a diabetic pump for my medication. A small needle delivered a continuous flow of the hyperemesis medication, instead of insulin for diabetes, into my leg. Even with the pump and the oral medication to keep my sickness under control, I had to be closely monitored because I was becoming seriously dehydrated too quickly.

The real test came in July. By the start of the month, I thought things were looking better. After a week, I felt like I might be pulling out of the morning sickness.

Then in mid-July, I had to call my mom because I got some pain in my side that caused my sickness to get worse. My mom took me to the emergency room. Not only was I severely dehydrated, I had developed gallstones as well. The doctors said the stones were small, and I would have to "live with them" because no one would do anything for stones that small, especially since I was pregnant. I was given a lot of IV fluids to get me rehydrated, and after several hours, I was sent home. It was about three in the morning when I got there.

At home, I went to sleep. I was instructed to call my doctor the next morning. So, I deliberately woke up at seven o'clock. When I explained the situation, I was told to come in right away. My appointment was at eight. I called my mom, who agreed to drive me.

As I opened the door to my house, I found my husband's stepbrother's girlfriend standing on the porch. I remember looking at her in surprise. "Um, hey Sarah, now's not a good time. I have to run to the doctor."

"Actually, that's why I'm here. Matt called and told us what was going on. He said you needed some help and asked if I could come by." Sarah was a woman on a mission.

I looked back toward the stairs. Angel was upstairs, slowly getting dressed. "That would be wonderful. I have to go to the doctor for a follow-up after the hospital visit," I explained calmly. I was exhausted. It had been a long night. I knew I looked like a mess, and I felt awful.

"Do you need a ride?" Sarah swung her keys around in her fingers. She was definitely prepared to help me out.

"No, that's ok. My mom is going to take me. She should be here any minute. But I know Angel is worn out. Would you mind watching her while I'm gone?" I'm not sure if my question came out as a question or as statement. My head was completely foggy from lack of sleep.

"I got it covered, and we'll clean while you're gone, too." Sarah smiled. Not long after she showed up, my mom arrived, and we immediately left for the doctor's office.

My doctor asked for a urine test, and the health problems I'd been having went from bad to a whole lot worse. I'd been given plenty of fluids at the emergency room, and within a few hours and absolutely no vomiting, my situation had gotten dangerous. When I did the urine test, I was horrified.

The color of my urine was mud. Mud! After getting several bags of intravenous fluids less than six hours before and sleeping from three o'clock to seven o'clock, both the doctor and I were shocked. She told me I needed to get to the hospital immediately.

I was checked into the labor and delivery floor, where they had a hard time finding a vein. My doctor came to see me as soon as she could. She said I was so dangerously dehydrated, my organs could start shutting down. The problem? The gallstones I was told I had to "live with" were causing me to be sick more than my body could handle, and more than the medication could manage.

My doctor gave me two choices: the first, do nothing and remain in the hospital indefinitely. The doctors and nurses would do their best to stabilize me and keep my baby and me alive. Neither of our chances were good with this option. My second choice was to have my gallbladder removed surgically. There was risk to my son, but my doctor told me I was right at my second trimester. This would be the time to do the operation because there was a good chance of saving my baby's life if he needed to be delivered early.

I'm sure some would say I had a third choice. I could have aborted my pregnancy to save my own life. However, that was never an option for me, nor even a thought.

I contacted my husband and told him what was going on. My husband was 4 hours away in Casper, Wyoming, when I was admitted to the hospital. He made the drive back to Denver in record time. He didn't care if he got pulled over along the way. Getting home was the only thing important to him. When he arrived, I was overjoyed to see him. He told me how he rushed back to town, and I was thankful he made it safely.

"Are you sure you want to go through with this?" he asked me after I told him I had decided to have the gallbladder surgery. I could hear the concern in his voice. He was worried for our baby and me, and rightly so. Both of us knew and understood the risks, but he trusted me to make the decision.

I held his hand and calmly told him, "I trust the doctor, and I trust God. Our son is strong and healthy. I know he'll be okay, and I'm strong."

I watched Matt's expression and knew no matter what I said, he was still going to worry. I squeezed his hand. "I have faith that everything will be ok, that God will protect us."

Matt gave me a nod; he respected my decision and knew that I wouldn't put either myself or our son in harm's way on purpose. "If you're sure, then I'll be here when you go into surgery, and I'll be here when you get out."

The decision to have the procedure came with some natural level of fear. However, I felt unnaturally calm and assured in my decision, as if there was nothing to really worry about. Everything inside me told me I was making the right choice.

Despite those calm feelings, I still began praying. I asked God to watch over and protect both my baby and me.

The next morning, I went into surgery. The procedure was done laparoscopically, so it involved small incisions, and it was less invasive than a traditional operation. Both my son and I got through the surgery well. They checked on him regularly during the procedure, and his heartbeat stayed as strong as ever.

I made a slow recovery, and I remained in the hospital a bit longer than expected. In fact, I was still in the hospital for my wedding anniversary, and my husband's company sent me flowers to wish me well. After that, my husband came back to Colorado to work. He wanted to be close to home in case anything else happened, and his company supported that. I was eventually sent home with a picc line so I could continue to get my medication. A week or two later, I had the line removed.

About two months after the experience at the hospital, I was able to get off the diabetic pump that dispensed medication for my hyperemesis. I felt somewhat normal again. I was thankful because I was struggling with the pump every day. The next time I got sick wouldn't be till my delivery.

In January, I delivered a beautiful baby boy. We named him "Dustin." I was grateful that my son was born healthy, with no ramifications from the pregnancy.

When I held Dustin in my arms, I knew I'd made the right choice. His tiny hands and feet, his precious face with that angelic smile, were God's way of telling me that I'd done the right thing. God trusted me to make the right decision, and I trusted Him to protect us. I gave my life and my son's life to Him, and He brought us through the danger we faced. Despite my fear, my faith in God is what gave me the strength to make the hard choice and the peace to see it through. I never would have been able to do that without God's help. I was never alone during that time. I had God with me. I trusted Him, and He provided me with the help I needed along the way. He even brought my husband home safely during the hospital incident and afterward to be by my side. God truly does provide for us when we give Him the control.

Never Alone

The Power of Prayer

Chapter II

"For where two or three gather in my name, there am I with them." Matthew 18:20 (NIV)

The power of prayer is amazing. Jesus says He is there with those who gather in His name. As a wife, it's my job to pray over my husband and to make sure my husband's needs are met, even if it means through prayer. I prayed for my husband often over the years, but not as regularly as I should have.

When we gather to pray for someone, God can do amazing things. It's as if our prayers become amplified when we come together. I once saw how powerful Jesus's statement about prayer really was. It involved a situation regarding my husband, and I reached out to members of our church for their help. We prayed and waited, and the results were truly a testament to Jesus's words.

For our whole marriage, Matt has worked as a heavy equipment mechanic. He has worked on construction sites in all kinds of different situations. He has worked in bad weather, on mountainsides, and late at night. Matt is a thorough and talented mechanic. He takes the time to make sure everything is done well and safely.

However, sometimes accidents happen that are beyond anyone's control. I used to worry about my husband when he went to work and honestly, I still do. I knew then, as I know now, the dangers in what he does. Over the years, I've heard horror stories about people getting seriously injured and even killed. Working on heavy machines isn't easy, and it's dangerous. For years, Matt had been lucky while doing his job. Unfortunately, all that changed one day, and my fears became a reality.

In 2016, Matt was working on a machine in the mountains. He did everything he was supposed to do to prepare for the work that needed to be done. He disconnected the battery to ensure there was no power to the machine. He even let the machine sit for a while before he touched it. Normally, there's no one around when Matt does his job. However, someone was there this time, and I thank God every day the man was close by.

Matt was working on the machine he had prepped for repairs when there was a spark, and his left arm caught fire. He said when it first happened, he couldn't feel anything, but that quickly changed. He stepped around the machine and thankfully, that coworker was there. The man who he was working with that day happened to be retired military. That guy jumped into action to help my husband. In the chaos of the event, they both forgot there was a running river just a few feet away from them. Their only focus was getting that fire out--and fast. Matt's coworker successfully smothered the flames.

The nearest town was Estes Park. Matt was rushed to the emergency room for care. I was home resting when I got the call, since I had just had surgery on my back. It was rare for Matt to call me during work hours, so I wondered if he was checking on me because of my surgery. I was confused when someone besides my husband came on the line.

"Kelly, there's been an accident," the strange voice said. "Your husband was working on a machine. There was a stray spark, and his arm caught fire."

"Wait--what?"

"His arm caught fire. He's seriously hurt. We're at the emergency room in Estes Park. The doctor will call you when he has a moment."

The stranger hung up. I felt confused by what was going on, and it was just me and the kids home at the time. I remember being in total shock, completely beside myself.

I sat there waiting for the phone to ring for what felt like an eternity, but it was probably only a few minutes. When my phone rang again, it was a nurse. She told me a doctor wanted to talk to me. I don't know if it was the shock or complete disbelief about what was happening, but I simply responded with, "Okay."

The doctor got on the phone with me, and the next thing he told me left my head spinning. "Your husband's whole hand and arm caught fire. We can't help him here in Estes Park, except to keep him comfortable. I'm going to have him transferred to a burn unit in Greeley. We're not sure at this point if his hand can be saved."

Numbly, I said, "Thank you for your time, doctor. Please let me know when you're going to move my husband"

Then I hung up the phone. A moment later, it rang again, and I answered, still numb. I could hear Matt in absolute agony, screaming as he told me not to drive up the mountain. He told me to get in touch with someone we knew to see if I could find a ride.

"Matt, I'll wait to find out where you're going, I promise." I tried to sound calm. "I won't leave without a ride."

After I got off the phone, I broke down in tears. My heart hurt. I didn't know what was going on with my husband, and I didn't know what would happen to his hand.

As soon as I could calm down, I called my father-in-law. When I filled him in on what had happened, he told me he was on his way to my house. I called my sister-in-law and my family and told them the whole story.

After I made my calls, my phone rang again. The nurse in Estes Park said Matt was in an ambulance and on his way down the mountain. She informed me that I would be contacted when he reached the hospital in Greeley. The place he was going to was an hour's drive from my house.

I remember walking into Matt's room in the burn unit. I saw how he was in terrible pain, and his arm was wrapped up in bandages. As soon as I saw him, I released a breath I didn't know I was holding. From the moment I got the first call, I was scared, worried and anxious. I cried, I prayed, and while I waited for information, I somehow calmed down enough to think about what needed to be done. So, when I got to his hospital room, I was finally able to breathe.

Matt's stay at the hospital was difficult. His burns had to be scrubbed daily, and it caused him a lot of pain. The scrubbing, as painful as it was, allowed the nurses to get the dead skin off and promote healing. Eventually the doctor said he wouldn't lose his hand, for which I was grateful.

However, Matt needed a graft to replace the skin on his arm and hand. So, a date for surgery was set, and that was where the power of prayer came into play. I decided to stay at the hospital so I could be there with Matt when he had surgery. But I also reached out to members of our church, specifically someone whose husband knew Matt well. I asked if they could come to Greeley to be with me and pray while he had surgery, and they agreed.

The morning of Matt's surgery, two members from our church showed up and sat with me. We prayed the surgery would go well. We prayed the doctors would have success. I was calm, and mostly just an anxious wife waiting for the doctors to tell me my husband was awake and all right. But I had peace, knowing everything was going to be okay. I was also grateful for the company. I really believe Jesus was there with us that day.

The original plan was for a skin graft, but that didn't happen. Matt is so skinny, the surgeons decided against the procedure. Instead, they took advantage of the anesthesia to thoroughly scrub his burn. As a result, he had to get more anesthesia because he began thrashing while they scrubbed. Still, the surgery was a success.

Eventually, Matt came home. I had to learn to care for his wounded hand and arm and change the bandages daily. His hand has healed since that time, though the lines where the burn was are still visible.

God protected my husband that day. He placed the other mechanic there to help Matt put out the flames. Without his help, the injury could have been a lot worse, even fatal. So, I'm grateful for that.

God also oversaw Matt's healing and treatment. He guided the doctors in their work to ensure his hand and arm would heal. He oversaw the surgery, guiding the doctors to make the right choices for my husband. God provided me with rides to and from the hospital as needed and care for my kids when the incident first happened. He gave me peace and calm, despite my nerves being all over the place. Remember I am only human, so those emotions will be there, no matter what, but God helped me to keep them under control. God also provided the people to be with me during the surgery, and we prayed. Three of us were there that day, and I believe based on the outcome, Jesus was also there with us.

It's amazing the faithfulness of our God and what He can do. The blessings He gave us during that accident and afterward meant everything to me. My husband's company backed him one hundred percent and checked in on him while he was in the hospital. The outcome of the investigation was that static electricity in the air probably caused the spark which led to his arm catching fire. It was a freak accident. Nothing my husband could have done differently would have changed that. But God was there from the moment the accident happened all the way through to when Matt's arm finally healed.

Since then, I pray for my husband nearly every day, way more often than I used to. I'm working on doing it on a daily basis. God showed me His faithfulness, and it's my turn to show Him mine.

Seek Him and Ask

Chapter 12

*"If you remain in me and my words remain in you, ask
whatever you wish, and it will be done for you."*

- John 15:7 (NIV)

I shared what happened when I prayed for my husband after his
accident, but what about praying for my marriage? Praying for
our marriages is just as important as praying for our spouses. A
marriage is made before God, and it's something He deems
sacred. In fact, it's so sacred that there are many verses in the
Bible that talk about marriage. For instance, the Bible tells us
two should become one flesh. This means we are no longer just
man and woman, but one flesh in God's eyes. He says we are to
leave our parents to be with our spouses. He even gives roles to
the husband and wife.

In God's eyes, the husband is the head of the family. It's his job to protect his family and treat his wife as sacred. A husband is to honor his wife and not be harsh. He is called to love her as Christ loved the church and to give himself up for her. It even goes as far as saying that a man who loves his wife, loves himself.

Wives are called to be submissive to their husbands. But what does that mean? It doesn't mean we are to be slaves to our husbands. It means we support them, encourage them, meet their needs, and provide care for them and our children. We must trust in them and their leadership as head of our households. We can and should have active roles in our relationships, where we discuss issues surrounding our home and family with our husbands, but we are still called to be respectful and supportive of them. It also means we are to pray for our husbands, as that is the biggest way we can support them.

Sometimes, though, something happens within a relationship, and the marriage begins to fall apart. What do we do then? The answer is simple. We seek God.

God says if we ask, we will receive. If we seek, we will find, and if we knock, the door will be opened to us. When things get too big, when our marriages start falling apart, we have to seek God for His help and trust that whatever happens is God's plan. It may not always work out the way we want, but we have to trust that God has a plan for us when it doesn't. There is always the chance God will provide healing to a broken marriage.

It was 2017. I was unaware at the start of the year that things weren't going well. I was doing my best to support my family. I was working on a project at the time that I'd started years before. When I began, Matt encouraged me to give it a try. I knew it would take a lot of work, and it meant I had to grow in some areas. But I was determined to succeed. Unfortunately, it came with a price.

I had a job. It didn't pay much, but it was the best I could do at the time. So, I was working a real job and doing this project on the side.

Unfortunately, Matt and I still grew apart, although I wasn't aware of it then. I thought things between us were going well. In fact, we got a horse together, something we both worked hard for. But that didn't change the fact that my marriage was falling apart.

I started to notice Matt acting odd at the beginning of the summer. Something felt off, and I didn't know what it was. So, I watched him and noticed the way he was behaving. I got a weird pull to check his phone. I found out he was having an affair, and not just with anyone, but with someone from his past. I was shocked, and I kept the knowledge to myself. I wasn't sure what to say or do. Instead, I held everything inside.

From time to time, I would sneak looks at Matt's phone. I knew he was up to something, and I was right. I saw messages that made me the bad guy, calling me selfish and all sorts of names. At one point, I saw texts about lawyers and taking the kids from me. I couldn't believe this was the road we were heading down. The more I saw, the more worried and scared I became. I started praying as hard as I could. I prayed every day and night that something would change. I prayed that God would help me figure out how to save my marriage.

One day, I even found myself at my church. I went there hoping to talk to someone, but the church was closed. I felt devastated. I knew I was running out of time to save my marriage, if I had a chance at all. I remember sitting down outside the church, crying. I felt my heart shattering, my soul ripping apart. Before I knew it, I was on my knees, praying out loud for God to help me, to help my marriage.

"Please, God, I want to be a better wife," I sobbed. "If I haven't been a good wife, please give me that chance. I don't want to lose my marriage, Lord. Please help me save my marriage. I don't want to lose Matt. I believe he still loves me somewhere in his heart, God. Please show me what to do."

I knelt there and cried my eyes out and prayed for a long time. I could feel the heat of the sun on my back as my voice became horse. When I was done, I felt drained, but a lot calmer. I remember slowly standing up and walking to my car. I stopped for a moment and looked back at the church. At that point, the only thing I knew in my heart was that I had to trust God to help me and give me direction.

One night, Matt told me he would have to go out of town to pick up a machine, and that didn't add up. He never had to pick up a machine before and bring it back. I knew something was going on. So, the next morning when he was supposed to be leaving town, I got one last look at his phone.

He intended to meet up with the woman he was having an affair with at a hotel that day, and he made it clear that when he did, it would be the end of our marriage.

Something inside me told me I had to confront him. I was scared, not sure it would do any good. But I closed my eyes and prayed, "God, help me. Give me strength and the right words to say."

When Matt got done with his shower, I took a deep breath and confronted him.

It didn't go well at first. He turned everything on me, blaming me for his affair and yelling at me for looking at his phone. But as we talked, he told me how he planned to leave that morning and end our marriage. At the same time, he said there was a part of him that wanted me to find out. He wanted to get caught. Then he told me how the affair started and who the woman was.

We continued to talk, and a lot of hurt came out between the two of us. I asked Matt to give me a chance to make things right on my end. I asked him to give us a chance to rebuild our marriage. I told him if he couldn't do that, I wouldn't keep him from leaving. In the end, he decided to stay.

Matt called the other woman and told her he wasn't going to meet her. She got angry and started cussing him out and calling me every name she could think of. She accused me of manipulating Matt and told him if he wanted to stay with me, he deserved everything he got. The odd thing about the story was that the woman was gay. She was interested in girls. She only wanted guys when she missed what girls couldn't give her.

Matt and I spent the day together, and we talked. We agreed that things needed to change. We had both made mistakes that had gotten us to where we were in our marriage. I laid down some ground rules. I told Matt I was hurt and betrayed and that I would need time to rebuild my trust in him. He said he didn't want me looking through his phone anymore, but he understood that couldn't stop happening right away. Matt was hurting too, and I did everything I could to let him know I still loved him in spite of what had happened.

We both went to individual therapy, and when it was time, we started couples' counseling. I wish I could say the other woman was no longer in our lives, but sadly, Matt found himself repeatedly reconnecting with her, even after I asked him not to. More pain and betrayal happened over the next year, and to make the situation worse, it became clear the woman was only using Matt for what she wanted out of him.

The woman never really cared about Matt, but she manipulated him without mercy. When it suited her, she dropped him quickly and put him down at every turn. But as soon as she needed something, she would call him and play the victim. My heart broke for Matt because in spite of the way he had hurt me, he didn't deserve to be treated so badly. He deserved better, and I wanted to be better for him. The other woman didn't stop with him, though. She continued to try and make me look like the bad guy, despite the fact that I had chosen to forgive him.

I prayed every day, from the morning I confronted Matt, to the day we could finally move on. I prayed for healing in our marriage and for Matt to know I truly loved him. I prayed for trust to be rebuilt between us and for God to guide me in how to be a better wife. I prayed for Matt's strength and for his eyes to be opened to what was really going on. I also asked God to forgive Matt for breaking our marriage vows. I asked for that because as a wife, I'm supposed to lift my husband up in prayer. I believed God had already forgiven him, or at the very least, He was ready to do so if my husband would only ask. I also prayed the other woman would get out of our lives once and for all because I knew she was poison to our marriage, and our marriage couldn't heal as long as she was around. However, above all else, I prayed God would use our circumstances one day as a testimony to others.

It's taken time and a lot of hard work on both of our parts, but God has healed our marriage. We still have rocky times. After all, Matt and I are both human. But we've come a long way. We listen to each other more, we communicate better with each other, and we're open and honest about issues that come up. We work hard to support each other, even if we don't always understand or like what we hear. Truthfully, we're still a work in progress.

I've trusted God every step of the way. Even when the devil whispers in my ear that I can't trust Matt or that he's up to his old habits, I've chosen to trust both God and Matt. I ask for God's help to keep from going down that road, and if something is really bothering me, I do ask Matt about it. He understands now when it comes up, that questioning him may be something I do from time to time. But he's being supportive and understanding. He knows he made a mistake; he knows he was wrong, and he knows he made many other mistakes as well. But so do I. I don't count myself blameless in what happened. If I want my marriage to work, I have to make changes to be a better wife to my husband.

God heard me that day when I cried out to Him at the church. I went to Him and sought His help. I wouldn't have had the courage to confront Matt that morning when he was about to leave if God hadn't been with me. I wouldn't have had the courage to stand by Matt through every step of the long healing process if God hadn't been there. God healed my marriage, and I believe He is still working on Matt and me. Marriage constantly takes work, so there will never be a perfect union between human beings.

Matt and I both wanted to fix our marriage and make it succeed. If only one of us had been committed to the healing process, we probably wouldn't have stayed together.

Some might ask why I stayed, since many people who are unfaithful once are likely to stray again. But God made us one flesh. God put us together. I was right when I believed Matt still loved me. If he didn't, he would have left that morning I confronted him. Ultimately, if our marriage was to end, the decision had to come from Matt and not from me. He chose to fight for our marriage. Because of that, I'll stand by my husband and defend him against anyone who speaks ill of him. God made the decision to keep us together, and who are we to question God's judgment?

Infidelity happens every day for others, and while I can't promise everyone will have the same outcome I did, I can promise God will be there. Ask Him, seek Him, knock on His door. Then trust Him to answer. He will help you and guide you. He will give you strength to confront your Goliaths. He will give you peace when you need it. He will heal you, and He will love you through your battles.

There are times when marriages will end, either because one or both parties choose not to work their problems out or because someone's safety is in jeopardy. In those situations, God has a plan. He doesn't want us to be unhappy or hurting. He would never ask any of us to stay in marriages or relationships that are dangerous or harmful for us. Whatever path God wants you to take, He will let you know, and He will guide you through your trials.

With that said, the devil knows how to prey on us and find small holes in our lives to dig into. That's why we need to be in a relationship with God over the long haul. God is the only one who can help us when our lives get out of control. He offers us the strength we need to step forward, the courage to face our problems, and only He can heal us. Only God is powerful enough to mend broken hearts and wounded souls. Only God is powerful enough to put shattered marriages back together. All we have to do is ask, and if we abide in Him and it's His will, it will be done.

Never Alone

Healing through Strength

Chapter 13

The LORD is my strength and my defense; he has become my salvation. – Psalm 118:14 (NIV)

I've shared about plenty of different parts of my life in which God has been faithful through my struggles. The next part of my journey happened in 2018, and this time my health was attacked.

In 2017, Matt and I got a horse together, a beautiful bay (brown) mare with white on her feet and on her forehead. Her name is Tally. She has a lot of spirit and has always needed an experienced rider who knows how to work with her. Like most animals, horses bond with people, and they always choose one person they will connect with. Tally chose my husband as her person.

In 2018, I didn't have a horse of my own, so I had to ride Tally. I was still learning how to ride. I could walk and trot, but I hadn't gotten the hang of cantering yet. In the Spring of 2018, I found out about a drill team tryout happening not far from me. A drill team is where riders do patterns on horseback, kind of like synchronize swimming, only in an arena instead of a pool.

I was interested in going to the tryout to watch and learn. I wanted to be on a drill team one day, but I knew I had a lot of work to do first.

However, I was encouraged by someone we knew to take Tally and go try out anyway, even though that was against my better judgment. Reluctantly, Matt and I loaded Tally up in a horse trailer and took her to the tryouts. When I got there, I told the other members I wasn't a great rider, and I was hoping to learn more about the drill team, so I knew what riding skills I needed to concentrate on. They welcomed me to the tryouts anyway and told me to do what I could.

I participated in part of the tryouts, and afterward, I was asked to join what was called a "practice team." A practice team was for those who wanted to become part of the team one day but weren't ready yet. Members were still required to meet at each drill team practice, and after the drill team had their session, the practice team would ride. The point of the practice team was for the riders to improve their riding skill. So, I thought it was a great idea. I accepted the invitation and began showing up for practices each week.

I had only been a part of the team for a few weeks when the first accident happened. I decided to ride Tally at a canter. My first attempt didn't go well, and my second attempt ended with me falling off and landing hard on the ground. I got up and noticed my ankle was hurting, but I thought I had just sprained it, and I didn't pay much attention to the pain. I was more worried about Tally than myself. I was relieved to know she was okay. After checking on her, the next step was to get back on. It was my choice to do so. I knew if I didn't get on right away, I would be too anxious the next time. That was the best choice I ever made, and it would prove to be a motivational tool later.

I went home that day with a very sore ankle. There was no bruising or swelling. It just hurt to put weight on it. I was told I might have fractured it, but I didn't listen. My body has always been weird. I've sprained my ankle many times before, and it never swelled and most times, it never bruised. So I thought I was okay.

I hobbled around for almost a week before my ankle finally started to swell and bruise, and the pain got worse. I decided to see a doctor. I had indeed fractured my ankle. I was given a brace and told to be careful and let my foot rest. A few weeks later, I was able to ride again.

On the morning of my first practice back, Tally wasn't herself; she was completely high-strung. The wind blew hard, and the temperature was a bit cold. Matt and I decided to load her up and take her because attendance was mandatory. However, if I could live that day over again, I would skip practice and stay home.

My first thought was that we would work Tally when we got to the fairgrounds, and she would hopefully calm down. But when we pulled into the parking lot, I noticed that every safe place we could work her was already in use. Normally, I would lunge Tally to help her relax and burn off some of her energy, or I would let my husband ride her for a short time if need be. I had some anxiety about riding Tally when she wasn't worked because to be honest, she's way more horse than I can manage. So, working her first gets her ready and safe for me to ride. But I figured I had to get past that anxiety of mine someday, and for whatever reason, I picked that day and ignored my instincts.

Once I got in the saddle, I talked to Tally softly, reminding her everything was okay. We got into the arena, and things were going well. I kept talking to her, and we took it slow. Tally was doing a great job, and I was proud of her. Then I started getting hot in my jacket.

Tally had never had an issue with items getting handed off to other people from her back in the past. Matt had done it several times. So, I didn't think it would be a big deal. I also thought she was in a good space because we had been doing so well.

I slid my right arm out of my jacket. The last thing I remember was switching arms to do the same with my left. My plan was to hand my jacket to Matt, who was in front of me at the far end of the arena.

I was told later that I had gone to hand Matt my jacket, and Tally spooked. She cut back and took off at full speed to the other side of the arena. People yelled at me to drop the coat, but I didn't. I vaguely remember trying to one-reign stop Tally, but not managing to do it. A one-reign stop is when you pull on one side of the reigns, turning a horse's head in toward its shoulder and your leg. The pressure is supposed to make the horse stop, but Tally kept right on going. Truthfully though, I don't know if I actually pulled on the reins or if my mind was playing tricks on me. The next thing I was told was that Tally cut back again, and that was when I flew off her back.

I couldn't see anything. I could hear voices. I could vaguely feel the paramedics moving me, but I saw nothing. Just darkness. Absolute black.

The next thing I remember, I woke up in the ambulance. I looked up, feeling confused and disoriented. I spotted the paramedic In front of me.

"Hi Kelly. I'm Steven. You had an accident, and we're taking you to the hospital." As soon as he introduced himself, I lost consciousness again.

The next time I woke up, I was in the emergency room. I remember noticing my shirt had been cut and feeling disappointed about it. But that was the last thing I remember till I woke up again in a hospital room.

The accident had given me a head injury. I fractured several places in my pelvis and my hip. I couldn't walk, and I couldn't put weight on my legs. But the worst part was, I was terrified about what had happened. I even began talking about giving up horseback riding forever. I was worried about Tally. I hated myself for what had taken place, and I knew I was to blame.

I went into the hospital on a Sunday. That Wednesday, I was sent to a rehab center to learn how to walk again.

"You'll be here for two months," said a nurse with an overly happy smile as she checked me into the rehab center.

"No way." I shook my head adamantly. "I have a husband and kids to take care of. You people need to get me using crutches and stairs as soon as possible, and then I'm going home. I'll do physical therapy from there, but I'm not staying here for two months."

"But a person with your injuries—"

"Forget it. Just get me on my feet. That's all I need."

During my time at the rehab center, I fought with myself. A part of me didn't want to ever get on another horse. Another part of me wanted to ride with Matt. I wanted to do trail rides and picnic rides and enjoy small events with him. I loved horses and riding, but my fear was taking hold of me.

I began physical therapy the day after I was admitted to rehab. By the end of the week, I was using stairs and crutches. I was told I had made the fastest progress the staff had ever seen. Monday, a week and a day after the accident, I was allowed to go home. I continued physical therapy with a therapist who made house calls. I was on crutches for almost a month. Due to my lack of mobility, I couldn't leave the house. So, I started painting to give myself something to do.

I began watching horse shows and movies, and one particular movie caught my eye. The movie was called "Walk, Ride, Rodeo," and it was the story of Amberley Snyder. I won't give the plot away, but it's an amazing story. As I watched the movie, I realized if Amberley Snyder could go through everything she did and still get back on a horse, so could I. Between watching that movie and fighting with myself, I made the decision that I was going to ride again, no matter what it took.

As always, I prayed during that time. I prayed about the accident and about what to do afterward. I was ready to let go of an important dream and goal of mine, but God didn't let me give up. He helped me get back on my feet, and I believe He put that movie about Amberley Snyder in front of me. He also gave me the determination to ride again.

I was cleared to ride later that summer, and I got back in the saddle. It was the hardest thing I ever did. I cried like a baby, but Matt was right there with me. I got back on Tally with Matt leading her in the round pen at a walk. I eventually started riding a friend's horse because riding Tally was too triggering for me. The accident wasn't her fault, and I never once blamed her, but the memories were enough to create a fear in me that wouldn't go away.

Since the accident, I've been on Tally a few more times, each time with Matt leading her, until I begin to feel nervous and then I get off. Only once since that day have I ever ridden Tally without him, when he was at a gymkhana event with a friend. I rode Tally next to that friend, without assistance from Matt. Also, since that time, I've helped care for her, from everyday grooming and feeding to tending her when she got hurt. While I may not be able to ride her like I did before the accident, I get a lot of joy from taking care of her and loving on her.

God put Tally in our lives, and later He gave me Arrow, my horse. Arrow was the most amazing first horse anyone could ask for. When I got him, he hadn't been well taken care of. That was something I discovered after we purchased him. However, I gave him the best life he could have ever wanted.

Arrow trusted me, and it was evident in our time together. He would always meet me at the gate or his stall door. He loved to rub his head against my back. The most important part was when he got a little spooked, he would calm down for me the minute I said, "I got you, you got me, remember?"

Arrow was an older horse, and he got me riding again. I almost started to canter with him, but we never made it that far. Unfortunately, I lost Arrow in 2022. He developed an infection in his hoof, and given his age, letting him pass was the best decision I could make for him.

God reminds us not to give up. He gives us the strength and the courage to move forward. I never would have gotten back on a horse if it weren't for God. He placed that movie about Amberley Snyder in my lap, and between that and my own convictions, I made the decision to ride again. He also helped me face my fears after I started riding. Every time I felt any nervousness, I would pray, and God would answer.

I also never would have found Arrow if I'd given up on my dream of riding. Arrow needed an owner who would take good care of him, and God had a purpose for me. I helped heal Arrow, and Arrow helped heal me. God knew we needed each other, and He brought us together. It was why Arrow responded to me the way he did, and it was why I could always be so calm with him. God's strength helped me to mend, both in body and spirit.

Ultimate Healer

Chapter 14

He said to her, "Daughter, your faith has healed you. Go in peace and be freed from your suffering." – Mark 5:34 (NIV)

God heals, not just our minds and our souls, but our bodies as well, if it serves His plan for us. He can provide healing to us, much like when Jesus healed the blind and the sick. Of course it looks a little different now, but God can still heal us.

You may have prayed, and you haven't been healed. Maybe the doctors have told you there's no cure for your health issue. So, perhaps you think God must not care about you, since He hasn't healed you.

First, being ill or injured can feel frustrating and suffocating, and believing God doesn't care about you can make those feelings worse. But the idea that God doesn't care because He hasn't healed you yet is a lie. God hears your prayers, and He cares about you more than you'll ever know. You are HIS child.

Second, God knows you can do so many amazing things with what you are going through. Your test can become *your* testimony for others. God knows who all of us will encounter in life, and He prepares us so we can be a light for those who may need Him. He takes our hardships and turns them into blessings, not just for us but for others.

Remember, the devil is against us at every turn and in every thought and action. The devil's purpose is to destroy us and pull us away from God. But God can take those moments the devil puts on us and turn them into real blessings if we allow Him to do so. Sometimes that means God heals us, and other times, that may mean He takes our health hardships and uses them for better purposes. It's up to us to trust that His plans are higher than ours.

Sometimes we have lessons to learn from our health difficulties, and it means we need to slow down and listen to God. Perhaps we aren't relying on Him enough, or perhaps we need to learn patience. Maybe we ought to practice humility and start leaning on others a little. Or there could be some other lesson God is trying to teach us. The only way we'll know is by spending more time in our Bibles and praying.

This may not make sense to you, but it's been my experience with many of my health issues. God has a plan that always works for our benefit if we have the faith to let Him do what He needs to do.

About seven months after my fall from Tally, I began to experience seizures. I'd never had seizures before, and I didn't understand what was going on. A few months earlier, I'd started my first job as a Paraprofessional for a Severe Significant Needs class in a local school district. I loved my job and looked forward to going to work every day.

I wasn't under any stress at the time. I had gotten back to riding. Matt and I were working through the problems in our marriage. At this point in my life, I was happy. So, I couldn't figure out what was causing my seizures. Truth be told, I didn't even call them seizures at the time.

The seizures were frightening. I didn't understand what was happening with my body. It was like I had no control. At first, I had what are called "Absence Seizures." A person checks out, much like daydreaming, but remains unresponsive for a duration of time. For me, the seizures would happen when I was talking to someone or when lights started flashing. I would have auras before the seizures. Auras are feelings or smells that sometimes precede seizures or migraines.

My auras consisted of a strange feeling of me going underwater from my neck up, or my fingers would start signing the first four letters of the alphabet back and forth in perfect speed. After I slipped into the seizure, I wouldn't hear anything. It was like I was blocked off, and my head would slump forward a little. When I came out of the seizure, I would jerk hard. Afterward, I would feel drained and confused for a while.

I immediately went to the doctor. At the time, I was on the school district's medical insurance, so I didn't have access to my regular doctor because of the type of coverage I had. The doctor I saw tried to tell me my seizures were psychologically based. He refused to give me any medication and referred me to a psychologist instead. I was given a small interview with a psychologist after I asked for a second opinion. The psychologist said he didn't see anything wrong with me, but that didn't stop the first doctor from giving me the diagnosis.

So, I went to my doctor's office outside of my coverage. I had to pay out of pocket for the full visit. After explaining everything to the doctor, she said I had a mild TBI (traumatic brain injury) that I had sustained when I fell off of Tally. She gave me some medication to control the seizures and also to help with some headaches I was having.

Unfortunately, my seizures developed into grand mal seizures, the type where a person falls to the ground and has convulsions. I was really scared. I knew I could lose my independence. I could even lose my driver's license and have to give up riding. I prayed during this whole time. I didn't believe for one minute my seizures were psychological.

My grand mal seizures happened unexpectedly at Thanksgiving that year. One minute I wasn't feeling well, and I wanted to lie down. The next thing I remember, I was on the floor looking up at people. I had a few more seizures after that, and my body hurt all over after each one. But it was the one that happened at the emergency room that caused my doctor to put me on an epileptic medication.

I began the medication, and the next morning, I was seen by a neurologist. It was an appointment I had set up before, and it just happened to fall the day after I started the epileptic medication. The interesting thing about that visit was that I hadn't been on the medication for twenty-four hours yet. When I went to see her, the very first thing the neurologist did was shine a light in my eyes. That action triggered a seizure, and she immediately said it was a psychological seizure because the medication didn't stop it. She told me to stop taking the prescription, and I refused. I knew my body, and I knew I hadn't been on the medication long enough for my body to absorb it completely.

I chose to stay on the prescription in spite of what the neurologist said, and as a result, I stopped having seizures. I couldn't believe it. For the first time in months, I felt human again and in complete control of my body. It was a relief to have that feeling, even if it was due to the medication.

In January, I returned to the doctor's office that my insurance was paying for. I saw a neurologist there, and a co-worker joined me for the appointment. I showed the new neurologist a video of my seizures, and we talked about what I was experiencing. I told him I was on two medications at that time and that since starting the second medication, my seizures had stopped. The doctor felt it was possible my seizures weren't psychological, but he couldn't be sure. He wasn't willing to dismiss the original findings from the first neurologist. The medication was controlling my seizures. So, we decided to wait and see what happened.

I eventually got off the first medication my private doctor had placed me on because it made me feel paranoid and depressed. Once off the medication, I felt better. The second medication continued to keep my seizures under control.

I had a follow-up appointment with yet another neurologist and was told again that my seizures were psychological, and I needed to stop all medication because it wouldn't control them.

"Mrs. Leffler, the only thing that will stop your seizures is therapy," the neurologist said, barely looking at me.

"Well." I smiled. "If that's true, then how come, since I've been on this medication, the last seizure I had was in December?"

The doctor stared at me, shocked, and couldn't answer me.

Finally, he said, "Your seizures are psychological. If you want to take the medication, you can, but it's not going to help. You need to see a psychologist."

I declined and went on my way.

A few more months went by, and I had to be seen again. I was experiencing that same paranoid feeling from before. In addition, I had this odd feeling that it was time for me to get off the medication. I couldn't explain it. I just knew it was time to get off.

So, back to the doctor I went. I explained why I was there and what I wanted to do. At first, the neurologist was happy to hear the news.

"That prescription isn't helping you anyway, Mrs. Leffler," he said in a condescending tone. "Stop taking it. I'll put in a referral for a therapist right away."

I shook my head. "I don't need a therapist. My seizures aren't psychological. The medication has been controlling them, but I want to get off because it's making me feel depressed and paranoid. It's time for me to stop taking the pills. I think I'll be okay, but if I'm not, we can set another appointment to figure out what will happen next."

The doctor didn't like that at all, but he agreed to take me off the medication. This happened Spring 2019.

From the time the seizures started to the time I came off the last medication, I prayed for God to heal me. I asked God to give me back my life. I was tired of fighting with doctors, and I knew my seizures weren't psychological. I prayed my independence would return and that I would be able to get a horse and ride with Matt.

I believe the feeling I had about coming off the medication was God telling me it was time, that I didn't need the prescription anymore because there was no longer anything to treat. I never had another seizure, not one. I've even spent time around flashing lights since then, and I haven't had one episode. I got back to riding horses, and that was the year I got Arrow.

I can't begin to explain or understand why, but I know God healed me that year for a reason. The pain I felt from those events created fear and uncertainty in me. My seizures were caused by a head injury that wasn't properly cared for. I never received treatment for a concussion or a traumatic brain injury. No one even mentioned anything to me about head injuries, with the exception of my private doctor.

Instead, I felt alone and unheard by neurologists who told me I would have seizures for the rest of my life, seizures that could only be managed with therapy. Well, God had other plans. God showed that He is the ultimate healer.

Don't get me wrong. If I had thought for one minute my problems were psychological, I would have sought out a therapist. I've always willingly gone to therapy when necessary, but this wasn't one of those times.

That experience made me stronger. I realized, while I needed the doctors who helped me, what I really needed was God. I had to maintain my faith in Him to get through those health problems, and it was hard. Believe me, it was hard.

Not once did I ever blame God for what happened. Did I ask Him why it was happening to me? Sure! But I never blamed

Him. God used that time to strengthen my faith in Him and to give me a chance to continue with my life. I was never alone through my seizures, even though I did feel like I was at times. God was always there with me, walking with me, helping me, and showing me what I needed to do. He placed it on my heart to see my private doctor, and He let me know when it was time to get off the medication.

God strengthened my mental health years ago. To doubt my mental health again would be to doubt God and my faith in Him, and I won't question God, not like that. How can I question God, who loves me, protects me, and has plans for me? How can I question my faith in Him in that way, when God has done so much for me and given me strength? I can't do that, and I will always stand on that.

The next time your health issues start to become overwhelming and you feel like no one is listening, take some deep breaths and quiet your mind. Ask God to guide you and give you peace. Let Him be your strength and remind you of His love and faithfulness.

Finally, ask God for healing. Pray for Him to use this time to help you become closer to Him. God heals everyone differently, and it's usually never in the way we expect or want. However, it's important to trust that God will provide healing in the way you need, according to His plan. For me, God is my rock, He is my fortress, He is my eternity, and He is the ultimate healer in my life.

Never Alone

Provider and Protector

Chapter 15

"Therefore do not worry about tomorrow, for tomorrow will worry about itself. Each day has enough trouble of its own."

- Matthew 6:34 (NIV)

The Bible tells us again and again that God will provide for us. It says that God will protect us, and we should not worry. As humans, not worrying can be difficult. What we don't tend to understand is how God works in ways we don't see. He is always working behind the scenes to provide for us and protect us.

If you stop and think about it, how many times have you come close to being involved in a car accident? Or how many times have you needed money to take care of something, and out of the blue you get blessed? We experience these moments more than we realize, but we tend to miss them.

For many today, finances can be hard. Costs have gone through the roof, and paychecks don't seem to stretch as far as they used to. I can't tell you how often Matt and I have found ourselves in tight situations. Something breaks, a big medical expense happens, or bills pile up faster than the money comes In.

At one point, we were a single-income family. Now both of us are working, and sadly, we're still struggling. However, God has always provided for us. When we needed an extra couple of dollars, the money has turned up somewhere. Not that God is an ATM. There are times I've had to put off some bills for the sake of feeding the kids or paying the rent. But when it mattered most, God has come through.

Last summer, we were expecting a major heat wave. Just a few days before it hit, our air conditioner went out. Our house becomes a fire pit during the summer, and with three people and two pets, surviving a heat wave without an air conditioner isn't an option. I wasn't sure what was wrong with the air conditioner, nor was I sure how we were going to fix it. We didn't have any extra money at the time. However, that didn't stop me from asking God for help.

I found a local business owner to come take a look at our air conditioner. A small piece needed to be replaced, and the price was seventy-five dollars.

"Thanks." I smiled. "I'll be in touch as soon as I can."

But God had other plans.

The business owner looked at me in surprise. "No, I'm going to replace the part right now. You can't be in this house with no air conditioner in the middle of a heat wave." He was direct with his words and his intentions.

I shook my head. "I can't afford the repairs right now. Thank you for your offer, but I'll call you when I figure out the finances."

The business owner gave a small smile. "You call or text me when you get paid, and we can settle up then. It's only a seventy-five-dollar piece. It's not that big of a deal."

I stood there, shocked. My eyes were big. I couldn't believe the business owner had offered to do such a nice thing for us. After what he had said registered in my mind, I smiled back and thanked him.

God was at work. He provided someone who could repair our air conditioner, and just in time. He provided for my family then, but it didn't end there. When it came time to settle up, I texted the business owner and told him I had his money. I asked when he wanted to meet up.

Once again, God provided. The business owner told me not to worry about settling up. He said he appreciated my honesty. Then he told me to consider the repair a blessing. All he asked for in return was a good online review. I smiled to myself and thanked him and God for their gift.

Without wasting time, I went online and left his business a great review. God knew I didn't have the money to pay for the repair and that I needed the money elsewhere. He provided when my family needed it the most.

God has shown up when jobs haven't gone right. Matt is a great mechanic. He works hard and really is talented at what he does. However, he's gotten the bad end of the deal once in a while over the years. He has had good jobs, but for reasons that were important at the time, he's had to leave those jobs. When that has happened, he has gone from job to job. He's had a difficult time finding the right fit now and then, and those bad experiences have left their mark. He has been treated so horribly, he has lost sleep, he has doubted himself, and at times that doubt has carried with him even after he moves on. This has been the problem for the last several years for him. One of those jobs treated him so poorly that he still struggles with it even today.

He left his last job because the company wasn't giving him hours, and they were treating him poorly. He got offered a position at three different places, and I was praying that God would help him find a position that would support our family and that would be a good fit for him. Matt needed a job where he could stay long term, and he needed a place that would treat him with respect. I prayed for that.

As we looked over the three jobs, one in particular stood out. I couldn't explain why, but I knew he had to take it. It was a great opportunity for him, and it would be a long-term position. Matt wasn't so sure about the job, though. So, I told him the decision was his. In the end, he chose the position I felt strongly about, and I'm glad he did. The job was hard to get on with at the start, but it has proven to be a great fit for him. He's been treated with respect and is seen as one of the top mechanics in their organization, so much so that he was one of the few to be chosen to get some specific training.

God answered my prayers, and the pull I felt about that job turned out to be right. Matt's confidence has increased, and he now holds a position with more authority in the company. I couldn't be prouder of my husband, and I couldn't be more thankful to God for providing for us.

These are just some examples of how God has provided for my family when we needed it most, and some examples of how powerful prayer can be.

God has also protected us when we needed it. I recall one particular afternoon; I had my son Dustin in the car with me. He was little, and I had just bought meals for us at a local fast-food restaurant. I had a sudden urge to stop and check my bag to make sure my order was right, and it was. After I pulled out of the parking lot and turned toward the light, I stopped again.

Maybe I dropped something, or maybe I was fishing for something in the bag. Either way, I stopped a car length back from the light. The moment I did, two vehicles collided in front of me. A car coming from my left ran the red light and slammed into the one turning toward us. The impact was so hard, it shoved the car that ran the light in my direction. That car stopped just a few feet from me. I watched in panic and shock, realizing that had I pulled up to the light like I was supposed to, we would have been hit head on. God knew what He was doing. That urge to stop twice before the light came from Him. He was protecting both me and my son that day.

God does amazing things when we aren't looking. How many times has God provided for you when you weren't expecting it? How many times have you been blessed with a little extra money or help from someone when you needed it most? How many times have you gotten up late or gotten out the door slowly and lost your temper, only to find out that had you left when you wanted to, you could have been in an accident? These are just some of the ways God intervenes on our behalf.

A lot of times, we let our emotions take control. That's normal. We're human, after all. Sometimes we need to let that frustration and stress out. But God wants that stress and frustration. So, the key is to not dwell on it, but instead, when we have calmed down, to give it to Him. God doesn't expect us to be perfect. That's not possible, and He knows that we're going to be driven by those emotions at times.

The important part is, what do we do with those emotions? Do we focus on them and allow them to consume us? Or when we calm down, do we give them to God and trust He will see us through? The key is giving our emotions to God, letting Him have control and refocusing on Him.

The next time nothing seems to be going right, try letting God drive. Imagine giving Him the car keys, and picture

Him sitting behind the wheel while you move over to the passenger seat.

Let God carry your load. Trust Him to provide for your needs and offer you protection. God is there with us. He hears us and all things happen within His time. God does great things for us. We have to give our hearts to Him, our faithful God who loves us. Anything is possible if we just trust Him to fulfill His promises to us.

In Every Way Depend on Him

Chapter 16

Now may the Lord of peace himself give you peace at all times and in every way. The Lord be with all of you.

– 2 Thessalonians 3:16 (NIV)

My most recent trial has been the hardest one I've faced yet. I say this because it has broken me down, and yet I've come to see it as my biggest blessing. It's because of this trial I've realized how blind I was. It has shown me how wrong some of my own beliefs have been.

I've always prayed for others when necessary, but I used to hardly ever pray for myself. When I did, it was from a place to help others or my family. I felt that petitioning God for my own needs was selfish and greedy. If my health was bad, I'd never pray to get better for myself. I'd ask God to help me get better so I could take care of my family.

I've also struggled with reaching out for help. I always felt so independent, and having to rely on others was embarrassing for me. However, it has taken this trial to show me the truth.

As I write this, I'm still going through my trial, and it has flipped my world upside down. I work as a Severe Needs Paraprofessional, and I love my job. In addition to work, I've also been attending school for the last few years. My goal is to become a teacher. However, what happened in October of 2023 would begin a change inside me and a change in my relationship with God.

On October 12th, I was injured at work. A Severe Needs student punched me on the left side of my face. The blow hit me on the jaw, right at my ear, and caused me to black out momentarily. After I came too, I was disoriented. The punch also left me with a very painful jaw and a headache. I reported the incident and immediately was sent to see a workers compensation doctor. During my medical exam, I was told I had a concussion, something I was surprised to hear.

I was instructed to go home and rest. A few hours after getting home, I began to have concussion symptoms. Lights and sound started to bother me, and I became very lethargic. When I went to get a drink, I discovered that everything was spinning.

I couldn't walk or balance on my feet. So, I had to crawl back into bed and lie down instead. My headache got much worse.

Within a few days, I started to forget things, such as what I was writing for my midterm paper and the material I had just read in my classes. I also began having issues with my words. I would be in the middle of a sentence and suddenly forget a word. It would take me several moments to remember the word before I could finish my sentence.

My speech was also affected. Sometimes I tried to say a word and couldn't. For example, if I wanted to say the word "Monday," it would come out instead as "Mmmmmm." Other times, when I would try to say a word, my mouth wouldn't work. An example of this was when I wanted to say the word June and as I tried to say it, my mouth just stopped working.

My processing speed began to slow and fail me, and I couldn't think correctly. I felt like I was in a fog, or that everyone was moving at lightning speed around me while I was stuck in slow motion. Whenever I tried to write, I began to miss words in my sentences, and I made a lot of terrible spelling mistakes.

My condition was making it hard for me to function, but the worst part was the difficulty walking. I had to rely on my husband and my son to support me any time we went out, which wasn't often.

I had an MRI to make sure there wasn't an injury to my brain. Luckily my MRI was clear. But that didn't mean I was out of the woods. I knew from my past experiences that a clean MRI didn't rule out a mild traumatic brain injury.

I was referred to a Concussion doctor, where I found out my previous head injuries, including the mild traumatic brain injury I sustained when I fell off of Tally, would complicate things for me. Repeat head injuries make it harder for a person to heal every time, and each one can create worse symptoms than before. It was explained to me that sustaining repeat head injuries is like having pneumonia. Once you have one, you're more susceptible to getting another, and the more you get, the worse they can be.

I was also referred to physical therapy, in hopes it would help restore my balance and reduce the severe dizziness I was experiencing. I was sent to a pain doctor for my headaches and a psychiatrist, who was supposed to evaluate my cognitive difficulties. Unfortunately, the cognitive evaluation didn't happen, and what came of that visit has been hindering me ever since.

The psychiatrist refused to do a cognitive evaluation. Instead, he tested only my attention and my memory. He interviewed me as well to get some background information.

When his report came out, it was only 5 pages long. Three pages were about my interview, and the other two consisted of two paragraphs that summarized his "findings."

The interview section was my first concern. My words had been changed, and information I gave was left out. His findings were even worse. According to him, I had "conversion disorder," and my symptoms didn't match with that of a concussion or head injury. He did recommend I get a second opinion to confirm his findings, but otherwise stated I needed to be removed from workers compensation.

I knew that psychiatrist was dead wrong. Worst of all, I had that evaluation done at the height of my symptoms. As a result, there was no way that evaluation could have been performed properly. Plus, it appeared as if he actually copied and pasted what the main doctor had said instead of using actual sources about concussion symptoms to support his reasoning.

In December, when I tried to talk to the doctor in control of my case about the report, I got verbally attacked.

"Mrs. Leffler, you're under my care," the doctor said coldly. "I make the calls, you don't. I decide what happens, and when. As far as I'm concerned, your problems are psychological.

I'll give you till January, and then I'm going to remove you from Workers Compensation, whether you've made progress or not."

"But I can barely walk. I'm having headaches."

"Maybe you just don't want to go back to work."

All I wanted was to go back to work and to have my life back, but that wasn't how the doctor saw it. For obvious reasons, I got very upset by the interaction with him. I became so concerned over the matter, I reached out to several lawyers for advice, and I spent my time praying constantly.

Toward the end of December, I was sent back to work against the advice of the Concussion doctor. I was unable to walk through the halls of the school when I arrived, and I was eventually sent home.

I was also encouraged by people, both outsiders and those involved in my case, to find a lawyer. The more I heard their advice, the more it weighed on my heart and mind. I asked God to give me some sort of guidance about what I should do. In the end, I did get a lawyer, someone I felt would help me move forward.

When I had my revisit with the doctor, he ordered me to stop working again till after my VNG at the beginning of January. At that time, I began recording every appointment with him. I'm glad I did because I would later find out that what he said to me at my appointments wasn't the same thing he wrote down in his reports.

My VNG went well, for the most part. One test at the end couldn't be completed because I got very dizzy, and my eyes started moving uncontrollably. The doctor tried to do an alternative test in which she moved my head left and right in short, quick motions. Immediately after she stopped, I got even dizzier and slumped to the left.

Despite my reaction, my attending doctor told me the VNG was normal. The ear, nose, and throat doctor, however, told me in a private message that she believed I might have post-concussion syndrome and a balance disfunction in my left ear. So, in order to be evaluated for the post-concussion syndrome, she referred me to a neurologist.

At one point, I was seen in the emergency room after passing out at a therapy session. After ruling out syncope—a loss of blood pressure to the brain--the emergency room doctor also said she thought I had post-concussion syndrome. My attending doctor, however, did not agree with this diagnosis. When he wrote his report, he left out the post-concussion syndrome and stated that I was treated in the emergency room for syncope instead. He agreed to the neurologist visit, though, and pushed to have it happen in person.

The neurologist aggressively questioned me, rushed through the exam, and told me I had PTSD. When I tried to ask questions, he refused to answer and proceeded to harass me about giving me a second opinion. His report gave my attending doctor exactly what he wanted, a psychological diagnosis.

Right after the neurologist appointment, I began acupuncture treatment for my headaches. Thankfully, things started to turn around. My dizziness improved, and I began regaining my balance. Between the acupuncture and the vestibular therapy, I was finally making progress toward getting my life back.

As of this writing, I am still struggling with cognitive processing, and walking consistently for more than thirty minutes is difficult. But I'm improving. I asked my attending doctor for a second opinion about the psychiatric recommendation, but my request was denied. So, I've started Cognitive therapy, paying for it out of my pocket. The therapist did an assessment, which showed a serious cognitive deficit. This assessment proves that the psychological diagnosis was wrong and supports the fact that the issues I'm experiencing are related to my head injury.

My case has finally closed. My lawyer has been amazing. The small settlement I got has helped pay for my medical care so I can continue to improve.

God has been faithful and guided me every step of the way through my health trial. He has given me the right words to say to the doctors, so I stay true to myself and true to Him. He has brought the right people into my life to help me get my problems fixed. He has also showed me that it's okay to pray for myself and to rely on others, two things I struggled with at one point. I've felt ashamed about relying on people, including strangers, to help me. He has shown me I don't need to be embarrassed. He has given me the peace I need about accepting help and willingly being open to it.

Every success I've had has been because of God. From being granted the acupuncture and the vestibular therapy, to my lawyer winning the settlement and the cognitive assessment, God had His hand on everything. But most importantly, is God, once again, has been my ultimate healer. He has helped me to make the progress I've made.

I know God will continue to be faithful to me as I heal and move forward. As for my job and my schooling, I trust that God has a plan. He has shown me that I don't need to be strong all the time, and while I can be self-reliant, I can also depend on Him for everything in every way.

Complete Surrender

Chapter 17

Jesus replied: "'Love the Lord your God with all your heart and with all your soul and with all your mind."

– Matthew 22:37 (NIV)

When people think of the word "surrender" in relation to God, they tend to think they're losing something. There are those who may feel they have to give up who they are, their dreams, their path. They view their surrender as losing a part of themselves in a negative way.

I look at surrendering as something more. For me, complete and total surrender means giving up who the world and society says I should be. It means giving up my sin and never going back. It means giving God complete control of my life, so I can become who I was meant to be.

When we surrender to God, we give up all those things, but we gain so much more. We gain a path God has planned for us. We gain His love, mercy, forgiveness, and the promise of eternity with Him. We gain His peace to aid us through the hard times.

Surrendering to God doesn't mean we give up on our dreams, but that we embrace the dreams and the calling He has for us. We gain so much more than what we are trying to cling to.

In the midst of my current situation, I began painting on canvas. I started the process in November. At that time, I was stuck at home. I never did any of my painting with intention. I just took some paint and spread it on canvas. Mostly, I began attempting the paint pour method.

In truth, it probably wasn't the best time to start something new. But in a way, it was perfect timing because I could just take a paint of any color and pour it onto a blank slate. That technique didn't require a lot of thought or planning. I was trying something new, and I felt like my head was completely messed up. So, I figured placing random paints on a canvas and letting them spread was the easiest thing to do.

About mid-November, I suddenly found myself wanting to read my Bible, but I couldn't read yet. However, that didn't make the desire to read go away. In fact, it got stronger. So, I decided to order a prayer journal and a book that would help me go through the Bible in a year. I knew if I was going to be successful, I needed the right tools for my journey.

At the beginning of December, I began writing in my prayer journal. I also started listening to the Bible through an app on my phone, since reading the words wouldn't work. When I could tolerate it, I wrote in my journal. In my other book, I wrote down the Bible verses, chapter and verse number only, that stood out to me. I used the app on my phone to highlight those verses so I could go back and write them down later. I began my Bible journey with the book of Matthew, and by the end of the month I had gotten through the Gospels of Mark, Luke, and John.

I also continued painting while listening to worship music, and my paintings began to evolve. I used paint colors based on how the music made me feel. I even named the paintings when I completed them.

At this point, I realized something crucial. I had once again lost my way. I needed to get back on track when it came to my relationship with God. I had a deep desire to one day hear God call me "daughter." That desire has filled every part of my being since, and it hasn't changed.

I immediately prayed for forgiveness for all my wrong ways and decisions. I made some mistakes and sinned against God in big ways throughout the years. I never sinned intentionally, but I realized some of my beliefs were lies. I also made choices, telling myself I was doing the right thing but knowing deep down I wasn't. I wasn't afraid to admit my sin, but it's an amazing thing to be loved by a God who only wants our full surrender to Him, especially when He has gone to great lengths to remind us He still loves us, and He is still with us.

I asked repeatedly for God to forgive me. It wasn't good enough for me to ask just once. I felt lost, and I didn't feel like I deserved forgiveness, nor did I feel like I had it. So, I prayed for it every day, and I took steps to clean things from my home that weren't serving me. It wasn't good enough to simply pray for forgiveness. I had to get rid of items that represented things I shouldn't have been attached too.

I asked God to help me use my words, my thoughts, and my actions to reflect Him and give Him glory. I also prayed for both my health and help with my case.

On January 1st, I saw people sharing their New Year's Resolutions and words for the year on social media. I realized my word was "surrender." I also had a feeling that as much as I wanted to share my renewal with God, it seemed like the time wasn't right yet.

I think I wasn't supposed to share because God was and still is continuing to work on me. God has been trying to heal my spiritual life with Him. I get the feeling I'm not strong enough yet in my walk with Him to share. In order to help others, I still need to work on myself. But in the meantime, He will guide me. As a result, I stopped posting often on my social media, keeping my posts limited and not commenting on many posts. I made the choice to completely surrender myself to God in December.

Since that time, I've "read" through twenty-two books of the Bible. I've bounced around between the Old and New Testaments, listening to any books I felt drawn to. I've also started a painting project. I've noticed as I go through the books, I get the sense of a color related to each book. So, I created two canvases, one for the Old Testament and one for the New, and I've painted the different colors on the canvases to symbolize the books. I look forward to eventually finishing both the painting project and the Bible.

As part of my complete surrender, I've felt more of God's presence. I've asked Him to guide my words during my medical appointments, and He has. I've asked Him to give me peace when life has gotten rough, and again He has. To be honest, I still have a habit of immediately getting angry or upset when things go sideways, but I'm slowly getting better. I've also asked God to help me with my words and thoughts in general, as they seem to be something I'm struggling with.

As a result, I have become more mindful of the words I say, and I'm trying to live my life the way God wants me too. It hasn't been easy. I stumble and fall, but I quickly notice and try to rectify my mistakes. I'm not going to be perfect. I know I'll mess up, and I know my changes don't mean much. It's where my heart is that matters. However, I'm doing my best to keep my eyes on God, and He has been proving how faithful and patient He is with me.

I started this book during my health trial. I originally planned it out, but I've let God guide me on what and when to write. He has been in charge, and while I don't know what will come of this book, I know I want God to use it for His glory and purpose. This book is about my testimony, from the very beginning till now. I know there is someone out there who needs to read the words on these pages, and as I said at the beginning, I hope, if it's God's will, my story will help someone else.

Another outcome of my choice to completely surrender to God has been that I've felt peace beyond all understanding.

You know that peace we hear talked about so much? It's real, and it's amazing. The future is still uncertain for me, but I'm at a place where I'm completely at peace with it. I've calmed down more quickly than I usually have in the past, and I've gotten to the point where whatever happens will happen. I don't know what's going to transpire with my health, my job, or my schooling. But I'm trusting God on this. I'm giving it all to Him. I made this decision in December, and I'm choosing to stick with it.

I know God will provide. I know He is with me. God has been healing me every day. I'm still having health struggles, but I'm making progress. My choice to trust God has been the best decision I could have made. I am still working on myself as well, so I can be worthy of Him and so I can hear Him call me "daughter" one day. Complete surrender to God means experiencing His amazing love and peace.

Never Alone

Foundation of Rock

Chapter 18

"They are like a man building a house, who dug down deep and laid the foundation on rock. When a flood came, the torrent struck that house but could not shake it, because it was well built." – Luke 6:48 (NIV)

Throughout this book, I've shared my testimony with you about numerous situations I've dealt with and how God has always been there for me. Now I want to take a moment to talk about something really important. Again, this isn't about preaching to you. It's about sharing my story and my views. I'll never tell someone what he or she should or shouldn't do, nor will I ever force someone into a decision he or she isn't ready for. So, what you decide to do with the information in this book is up to you.

In the end, the decision to have a relationship with God is a personal choice. No one can force you into it, and most certainly no one should guilt you into it. Your relationship with God, if you choose to have one, has to be a complete surrender, because when you make that choice, you are literally giving God the steering wheel to your life. You are agreeing to turn away from all sin in your life in order to be closer to Him.

You are human, and you'll struggle. However, you cannot continue your old way of life if you want a true relationship with God. Therefore, the relationship will have more meaning to you if you *want* it for yourself and not because someone else has pushed you into it. Fact is, God desires for you to *want* that relationship with Him. The more personal that decision is, the more meaning it has, and the stronger your relationship will become.

It's important to know what makes a strong foundation in our relationship with God. I'll be referring to several Bible verses to support my view. You can find those verses and others listed in the back of the book. I encourage you to look them up and see for yourself what the Bible says.

Our relationship with God must be built on a solid foundation. Jesus tells us that a house built on rock is sturdy, while a house built on sand will crumble. (*) He uses this analogy to help us understand the importance of having a firm foundation in our relationship with Him.

The stronger the foundation, the stronger our relationship with God will be. We'll all face trials and find ourselves tempted during our walk. That strong relationship with God will help us to get through those moments, even when it feels like we can't. So, what makes a strong foundation in our relationship with God?

I believe a strong foundation is made up of three things. The first is the Bible. This isn't new information, but sometimes we need to be reminded of how important the Bible is to our walk with God. The Bible is God's word. It holds everything we need to know about what God expects of us as Christians.

There are three very important things in the Bible. The first is what God views as sin, or what has separated us from God. It's important to know what God considers to be sin. We can't turn away from what separates us from God if we don't know what to turn away from. Thankfully, the Bible outlines sin perfectly for us.

God views many things as sin. Some of those things are adultery, lying, stealing, worshiping idols, committing murder, and practicing homosexuality. (*) The Bible also talks about how important it is to maintain control of our anger. (*) God makes these things clear for us so we can better understand His will.

We have all worshiped "idols," even if we haven't intended to. Worshiping idols isn't always about creating gold alters or bowing down before false gods. Sometimes it's the celebrities we put above everything else, or even worse, the smartphones we can't look away from. These things can be idols in our lives.

What about adultery? Well, God says it's a sin, but most people think it only counts if you act on your feelings. However, Jesus said even thinking of someone in lust is considered adultery. (*) It's important to read our Bibles, so we can fully understand God's laws and make changes in our lives.

This brings us to the most important part of the Bible. While God's Word outlines what sin is, it also tells us about God's promises. It's our human nature to want to know what we get in return when we give up the old parts of our lives. While we can't have answers all the time, the Bible gives us access to this particular answer by telling us about God's love, peace, mercy, and faithfulness to us. We also find out about the ultimate gift God has given us, Jesus Christ, and the sacrifice Jesus made for us. We learn of the promise of a relationship with God and eternal life. We get to see God's promises come to life through the stories in the Bible, from Abraham to Job, from Daniel to the New Testament when God fulfills His promise of hope and protection through Jesus and the disciples. We need to cling tightly to these promises when things get rough in our lives. It's God's promises that will see us through.

Finally, the Bible lays out everything we need to know about what our relationship will be like. It talks about the persecution we will experience as Christians, and it tells us about what is to come. The Bible explains how we are to handle persecution and instructs us to take heart and have faith in the promise we have in God through Jesus. The Bible prepares us for the future, both here on Earth and in eternity with Him.

Everything we need to know is in the Bible. Reading God's word keeps us close to Him. Scripture gives us the chance to see what God deems as sin and not what the world wants us to believe. In the Bible, we find hope for the future and guidance to face what is to come. The Bible is the literal blueprint for our lives. The deeper we dive into Scripture, the stronger our foundation grows. We need the Bible in our lives. We need to take in God's word and let it nourish us. When we have God's word in our hearts, the views of the world cannot trick us into believing lies that will pull us away from Him.

Never Alone

Solid Ground

Chapter 19

"Therefore everyone who hears these words of mine and puts them into practice is like a wise man who built his house on the rock."- Matthew 7:24 (NIV)

The next two important pieces of our foundation are prayer and faith. Both will help to solidify our relationship with God. It's through prayer that we talk to God, and it's through faith that we trust Him in all things. It's important for us to have a connection to God, especially when we need Him. Our connection with Him reminds us we are not alone and that He is always there with us. We need our faith because we have to believe God will take care of us if we do our part.

The Bible tells us prayer should be done in private. (*) Prayer is an intimate conversation between us and God. Prayer helps us strengthen our relationship with Him. When we go to

God in prayer, we are laying our burdens at His feet and asking Him to intervene where we are struggling. Praying in private can be anything from writing in a prayer journal, speaking aloud behind closed doors, or even thinking silently while doing household chores. Quick prayers are great on the go throughout the day. They can help ground us and keep us focused on God. No matter how prayer is done, it's important to be honest, vulnerable, and open with God. In short, prayers need to come from the heart.

Using a prayer journal has helped me during my health struggles. For me, writing out my prayers has made them more intentional. Making lists keeps me focused on what I'm praying for. I also find it much easier for me to be fully open and raw with God in writing. A journal causes me to dive deep into the emotions I'm experiencing, in order to give God my struggles.

I've also prayed quietly in my head. I'm not much for talking out loud when I pray, but some people are. Those prayers, when done from your heart, are just as effective as written ones. I've personally found quick prayers are great when something comes up suddenly, but for me they lack that raw, intentional emotion I get when I write in my journal.

There is another form of prayer I find really helpful and packed with intention. It's when we pray with others about a situation. The Bible says that where 2 or more gather, there He will be. (*) In my story about Matt's accident, I asked for people from my church to gather with me during his surgery and pray. That level of prayer magnifies our intention to God. It's amazing to feel the presence of God when you pray with those who surround you in fellowship.

Faith is also important to our foundation. Faith—that's a big, powerful word. Jesus tells us if we have faith the size of a mustard seed, we can do anything. (*) People seem to think our faith needs to be big and overwhelming, but it doesn't. It can be small, and that alone is enough for God. Mustard seeds are tiny, and Jesus tells us if our faith is that big, we can move mountains! How amazing is that?

When we give God the steering wheel to our lives, we are choosing to take a leap of faith, and to allow Him to have total control. That can be scary because it means fully trusting God, even when everything is going wrong. Our faith, though, has the ability to get us through the toughest of situations.

With these three things--the Bible, prayer, and faith--we have the ability to strengthen our relationship with God. Reading our Bible gives us the confidence to know what God wants and what He provides. We can see His work happening in our lives. Prayer allows us to be intimate with God, to get on a personal level and have a close relationship with Him. We need faith so we can trust God. We have to believe that God will be there for us, to guide us in a way that will glorify Him as well as benefit us.

When these three things are in place, we create a strong foundation for our relationship with God, built on solid rock. The strong foundation allows us to withstand those trials we will most certainly experience in life. The Bible, prayer, and faith will keep us rooted in God's love and grace and help us to remain focused on Him, even when we feel ourselves starting to lose our balance.

I mentioned in one of my stories that I left the church, and I was away for quite some time before I returned. In that situation, I felt God wanted me to step away. However, I will always encourage people to attend church.

It's important, though, to understand that church isn't a building with four walls and a steeple. That's just a place. The Church is us, the people who gather in the name of Christ to worship Him and to strengthen our relationship with Him through our fellowship with each other. Many people believe Church is the place we go, that being in a building is important. I disagree. I believe what's important is our faith in God, following His laws and worshipping Him. What's important is our connection with each other and supporting each other in our faith. We need each other as fellow brothers and sisters in Christ, but we don't need four walls to have that.

As Christians, the path we walk is narrow. We face temptation regularly, and we find ourselves being attacked by the enemy often. So, it's important that we hold each other accountable in our journey. We need to remind each other that God is there for us and what God has called us to do. (*) We need to lift each other up when we're struggling, when we feel defeated or alone. We need to help each other stay focused on God. Having that encouragement can be a great blessing for us as fellow followers of Christ. Everything we do should be for the glory of God alone. If it isn't, then we aren't being the best Christians we can be.

Staying in a church where the members are treating people badly isn't mandatory. While we should hold each other accountable, sometimes that isn't possible. Some will turn away from that accountability. When we experience problems within a church as a whole that don't improve, moving on is an option.

Today we have become a society that worries about offending people. Sadly, some churches are concerned about insulting the world. They alter their message to keep from offending others, but in doing so, their message no longer aligns with God. These churches are so worried about offending people, they forget that Jesus didn't worry about who He offended. He upset a lot of people. Specifically, the Pharisees and Sadducees, the religious leaders of Israel at the time. Jesus flipped tables in the temple when he saw the poor being taken advantage of by businessmen and money changers. He broke the law by healing people on the Sabbath. (*) Jesus saw that neither the message nor the actions of the Pharisees and Sadducees aligned with the message of God. Unfortunately for them, Jesus didn't accept their excuses, and neither should we. So, leaving a church whose message doesn't align with God and finding a new one is a good idea. God knows where we belong. He wants us to become stronger in His word, not weaker.

Eventually, there will come a time when as Christians, we will find ourselves unable to attend church. We know the end of days is coming. The Bible tells us this will be a time of great tribulation, especially for Christians. When that time comes, we may lose our right and ability to read our Bibles and attend church. We should commit as much of the Bible as possible to memory now, while we can. We cannot make the church building our foundation, either. If we make going to a church our foundation, then when we are stripped of it, our foundation will crumble. We will need each other, and we will need to come together in different ways. When that time comes, our church will be each other and the relationships we have with both God and our fellow Christians.

A firm foundation in God is crucial. If our foundation is built on the Bible, prayer, and faith, we have a better chance of surviving the end of days. Connecting with others and building our church through our relationships will also help us to remain strong in our faith and walk with God when things get bad, and they will.

A connection with God is really important, now and in the future. Through that connection, we will remain strong in our faith and in our relationship with Him. We will find the strength to weather the storms of life. We will hear Him when we seek His help and keep Him near to us at all times. A solid foundation, built upon a rock, can weather any storm. A foundation built on sand will crumble. The question is, which foundation will you build your faith on?

Never Alone

Never Alone

Chapter 20

Be strong and courageous. Do not be afraid or
terrified because of them, for the LORD your God goes with
you; he will never leave you nor forsake you.

– Deuteronomy 31:6 (NIV)

"He will never leave you nor forsake you." God's word tells us over and over again we are never alone. Yet we find ourselves feeling alone at times, especially when things go wrong in our lives. However, if we root ourselves in God's word and keep Him close to us, we will find, even when the storm is raging or when the darkness feels like it's too much, God is always there with us.

Throughout the years, my trials have taught me valuable lessons. Even now I tend to lose sight of them, and God has to remind me of them all the time. I'm a sensitive person, and I tend to wear my heart on my sleeve. Despite that, my trials have given me many blessings and gifts including patience, love, faith, trust, peace, courage, hope, strength, clarity, and humility. Most importantly, though, they have given me testimonies to share with others.

I know God hasn't abandoned me. My faith is stronger today than it has been in a long time. My life hasn't been easy, but God has a plan. I can feel Him with me when I need Him most. I can't speak for God, but in my heart I believe He knows I need more reassurance than most, and He hasn't failed to give it to me.

I spend just about every night in my Bible. I pray every day, either writing in my journal or quietly in my head. Anymore, I listen to nothing but my worship music. For me, being closer to my heavenly Father has become my top priority. I have to remind myself when things get rough, that God hasn't abandoned me. He has been faithful to me every step of the way, and the best way I can thank Him is to remain faithful to Him in return.

Complete surrender has meant giving up myself to Him. It has been a relief to lay my burdens at the cross and in return, I have gained something more precious than anything this world could ever give me. I have gained a relationship with the one who truly loves me.

When I started writing this book, I had no idea how it would go. Initially, I thought it would end up like my many other unfinished book attempts. However, as I began to write, I found if I let God have control, the writing came to me almost automatically.

I originally had an idea of what stories I wanted to share with the world, but God had other plans, and several things got left out. Ok, a lot got left out. That just shows this is God's book, not mine. He knew what needed to be said; I only wrote it down. He has taken my tests and turned them into testimonies to share with others.

This book is meant to be a light for you, a source of hope during your most difficult times. If you find yourself struggling with anything similar to what I've been through, remember, God is always there with you. Your outcomes may not be the same as mine, but that's because God's plans for each of us are different. Still, no matter what, He will help you through the hardest of times. All you have to do is reach out for Him, lay your burdens at the cross and completely surrender to Him.

If I can find peace with God, you can too. If He can save a lost little girl in the darkness, He can save you. Just like His word says, God has plans for us. He wants us to prosper, to have a future and to have hope.

However, we have to go "all in" and give Him everything. That surrender doesn't mean you will be perfect, but that's the amazing thing about His love and grace. We don't have to be perfect. We just have to follow His word, have faith in Him, trust Him and give Him everything, and He will do the rest.

I know that can be difficult at times, but it's true. As you saw with my stories, God has been faithful through everything, even when I didn't think He was there. When we feel alone, He is still carrying us, even if we can't see it. God just wants us to trust Him completely.

When I think about faith, I think about Job and his story. You can find the book of Job in the Old Testament, and it's worth the read. Here's a sneak peek about him.

Job was a man who lost everything, and despite it all, he never lost his faith in God. Job's faith in God is the perfect example of the kind we need to have. We're only human, but we can work on having faith like Job's by remaining focused on God.

Nothing is possible with man, but everything is possible with God. God is the ultimate healer, the ultimate light, and He loves us unconditionally. God knows what our needs are, but He wants us to go to Him and ask. He needs to know we trust Him to step in and take control, that we have faith in Him to do what's best for us. God knows who is struggling right now. He knows there are those who need Him, and that's why He uses our tests as testimonies to help others.

We can't be afraid to humble ourselves and share our testimonies because they can help other people. I know it can be scary to share our stories, but if our testimonies can help others, it's worth overcoming our fears. Even as I'm finishing this book, my own nerves have begun. But I promised God that I want Him to use me as a testimony to help others. This book is a result of that promise. Now I have to trust Him as I move forward with it.

We have to trust that God knows what He is doing. God's message of hope and love is the most important message we can share. He knows who needs to hear it the most, and He brings that message to us in ways we will never expect.

My story isn't done yet. It's only getting started. Your story isn't done yet, either. It's just waiting to be written. Most importantly, God needs us to know and to always remember that we are never alone. You are *Never Alone*.

Never Alone

And now these three remain: faith, hope and love.

But the greatest of these is love.

– 1 Corinthians 13:13 (NIV)

For we live by faith, not by sight.

– 2 Corinthians 5:7 (NIV)

Never Alone

Bible Verses

On the following pages, you will find a list of Bible verses for your reference. Cross check them, write them down, or mark them in your Bible if you wish. I have listed the verses from each chapter first. After that, I have listed a few verses with topics related to that chapter underneath. Since there are sometimes many verses on one topic, I haven't included all of them. Instead, I've listed the ones I've felt led to share. I hope these verses help you on your journey, and you experience God's love and peace in a profound way.

Chapter Verses

Jeremiah 29:11	Isaiah 41:10
Psalms 147:3	Philippians 4:7
Matthew 14:31	Romans 8:28
Psalms 127:3	Galatians 6:2
Matthew 19:14	Psalms 91:2
Matthew 18:20	John 15:7
Psalms 118:14	Mark 5:34
Matthew 6:34	2 Thessalonians 3:16
Matthew 22:37	Luke 6:48
Matthew 7:24	Deuteronomy 31:6

Reference Verses by Chapter

Chapter 5

Peter, Jesus, and the Storm

Matthew 14:22-33

Chapter 12

Marriage

Genesis 2:24	Proverbs 12:4
Matthew 19:5-6	Mark 10:8
1 Corinthians 7:1-5	Ephesians 5:22-28
Ephesians 5:31, 33	Colossians 3:18-19
Titus 2:4	1 Peter 3:1,7

Chapter 18

Sin

Leviticus 18:23	Deuteronomy 5:1-21
Proverbs 6:16-19	Luke 18:20
Romans 1:29-32	Galatians 5:19-21
1 Timothy 1:8-11	Hebrews 10:26
1 John 3:15	Exodus 20:14
Proverbs 6:25-29	Matthew 5:27-28
Matthew 19:4	1 Corinthians 6:9
1 Timothy 1:10	

God's Promises

Exodus 14:14	Exodus 34:6-7
Numbers 23:19	Deuteronomy 1:30
Deuteronomy 3:22	Deuteronomy 31:8
Nehemiah 4:20	Psalms 4:8
Psalm 32:7-8	Psalms 33:12
Psalm 46:1	Psalms 121
Psalms 139	Psalms 146:6-7
Isaiah 26:3,12	Isaiah 41:10
Isaiah 49:15-16	Isaiah 66:13
Jeremiah 29:11-13	Matthew 7:7
Matthew 11:28	Matthew 19: 28-30
Matthew 24:13	Luke 6:35-36
Luke 11:9	John 3:16-17
John 11:25	John 14:1-7
Romans 8:28	2 Corinthians 1:3-4
Ephesians 3:16-19	Philippians 4:7
Philippians 4:19	2 Thessalonians 3:3
James 4:10	James 5:15
2 Peter 2:9	Matthew 5:3-12
1 John 1:9	1 Corinthians 10:13
1 Corinthians 15:3-4, 54-57	2 Corinthians 1:20-22

Faith

The Book of Job	Proverbs 3:5
Isaiah 40:31	Matthew 8:13
Matthew 9:29	Matthew 15:28
Matthew 17:20	Matthew 19:26
Matthew 21:21-22	Mark 5:34
Mark 10:52	Romans 1:17
Romans 5:1	Romans 10:17
2 Corinthians 5:7	Galatians 2:16
Ephesians 2:8	Ephesians 6:16
Hebrews 11: 1-40	James 1:3,6

Chapter 19

Prayer, Praying Alone, and with others.

2 Chronicles 7:14	Jeremiah 33:3
Matthew 6:5	Matthew 6:6-13
Matthew 18:20	Matthew 21:22
Mark 11:25	Luke 18:1-8
John 14:13	John 15:7
Romans 8:26	Romans 12:12
Ephesians 6:18	Philippians 4:6
1 Thessalonians 5:17	James 5:14,16

Jesus and the Pharisees, Scribes and Sadducees

Matthew 12:1-14	Matthew 21:12-17
Matthew 22:15-46	Matthew 23:13-36
Mark 11:15-19	Luke 13:10-17
John 8:13-59	

Never Alone

Acknowledgments

There are several people I'd like to acknowledge and thank for their support and encouragement, both now and throughout the years.

First and foremost, this book wouldn't have been at all possible without God's blessing and guidance. I'm grateful to Him for giving me the words during my writing process. I'm also grateful for everything the Lord has done for me throughout my life. I'm who I am today because of His faithfulness and love. I know I'm still a work in progress, and I continue to pray that God will mold me into the woman He has asked me to be. I also pray that one day I will be able to hear Him call me "daughter" as He says the words, "Well done, my good and faithful servant."

Next, I'd like to thank my family, starting with the most important person in my life, my husband. I love you so much; you are my rock and my biggest supporter. Thank you for your love and encouragement and for walking this life path with me. To my children, I love you both dearly. Despite the obstacles you have faced, I'm proud of both of you for who you're becoming. You'll always be my Angel Girl and my Bubba. To my parents, I love you both. I'm the person I am because of your guidance and discipline. I know we don't always agree, but I'm grateful for your love and support. To my sister, you'll always be my baby sister. I love you, no matter what. Thank you for being there for me and for your niece and nephew.

I appreciate the positive influences in my life, including my teachers from third through seventh grade and my favorite English teacher in High School. Thank you to all of you for helping a little girl heal and realize her potential. You believed in me when I didn't believe in myself. You gave me the courage to stand up for myself and take risks. You gave me a voice and a passion for helping others. I'll be forever grateful to you all.

My friends are the most amazing people a woman could ask for. I don't have many, but it's the quality that matters. Dayna, Charisse, Chris, and T.D., you've stood by me through a lot of ups and downs. You've given me strength, a listening ear, and a shoulder to lean on when I needed it most. You've prayed for me and supported me when I've felt lost. Friends like you are truly more precious than gold.

I can't forget the amazing group of writers in Brighton, Colorado, who have supported me, encouraged me, and helped me on my journey. I'm forever grateful for their guidance. They've taken the time to help me shape and edit my book. They've given me amazing feedback, and I've been blessed to have the opportunity to learn from them.

Finally, I'd like to thank a friend of mine. This friend encouraged me to move forward with this book and my companion books. She has reminded me that God has a special purpose for my books and me. So, to my friend Brooke, thank you for urging me to take a leap of faith. Thank you for reminding me that God has plans for all of us, even when we don't think we're brave enough to take the first step.

Never Alone

About the Author

Inspiring Hope through Faith

K. M. Leffler is a Christian mom and wife who lives in Colorado. She is dedicated to her journey with God, and believes in God, family, and work.

Leffler has a heart for helping other people, writing, and getting closer to God. She has overcome obstacles in her path and believes that with God, anything is possible.

As a Christian, Leffler believes that a relationship with God is important and therefore has a strong desire to share her faith with others through her testimony.

Her goal is to help others find peace and hope in their lives. Her hope is that through this book, others will come to know God and experience His amazing love and mercy in their lives.

It is for this very reason that she believes that when we find hope, we discover our faith and it is through our faith, that we can embrace love through God's and His promises.

SIGN UP FOR MY
AUTHOR NEWSLETTER

Be the first to learn about K. M. Leffler's new releases and
receive a free gift and exclusive content!

www.kmleffler.com

.